# Ga

## *The Story of a Genocide*

Edited by
**FATIMA BHUTTO**
and **SONIA FALEIRO**

**VERSO**
London • New York

First published by Verso 2025
© Verso 2025

Chapter 2 first published as the new introduction to Tareq Baconi's *Hamas Contained*
Chapter 3 first published in *Protean Magazine*
Chapter 4 first published in the *Baffler*
Chapter 7 first published in the *New Yorker*
Afterword first published in the *New Arab*
"Gaza Reflections" first published in the *Comics Journal*

The manufacturer's authorized representative in the EU for product safety (GPSR)
is LOGOS EUROPE, 9 rue Nicolas Poussin, 17000, La Rochelle, France
Contact@logoseurope.eu

3 5 7 9 10 8 6 4

**Verso**
UK: 6 Meard Street, London W1F 0EG
US: 207 East 32nd Street, New York, NY 10016
versobooks.com

Verso is the imprint of New Left Books

ISBN-13: 978-1-83674-224-1
ISBN-13: 978-1-83674-226-5 (US EBK)
ISBN-13: 978-1-83674-225-8 (UK EBK)

**British Library Cataloguing in Publication Data**
A catalogue record for this book is available from the British Library

**Library of Congress Cataloging-in-Publication Data**
Library of Congress Control Number: 2025941401

Typeset in Fournier MT by Hewer Text UK Ltd, Edinburgh
Printed and bound by CPI Group (UK) Ltd, Croydon CR0 4YY

# Gaza

# Contents

# Preface

In January 2024, we launched a fundraiser for children who lost limbs in Israel's attack on Gaza—an area now home to the largest cohort of child amputees in modern history. According to Reuters, the number of known child amputees in Ukraine after nearly two years of war was thirty. In Gaza, in just about two months it was over 1,000, according to UNICEF. Our initiative, launched with Julia Churchill and called #BooksforGaza, united writers, editors, and publishers worldwide. Together we raised over $85,000 for The Ghassan Abu Sittah Children's Fund, which brings children out of Gaza to Lebanon for reconstructive surgery. The number of child amputees continues to rise. Palestinian and international doctors have spoken about children not only being maimed by the Israeli army, but also deliberately killed by snipers—shot in the head. The sheer number of child deaths in Gaza surpasses those of any recent conflict—Ukraine, Syria, Iraq, Afghanistan, and beyond.

Amnesty International has called Israel's campaign

against Gaza "genocidal." The organization found that Israel

> committed acts prohibited under the Genocide Convention . . . by (imposing) conditions of life calculated to destroy Palestinians in Gaza through three patterns of events: the wide scale damage and destruction of critical infrastructure and other objects indispensable to the survival of the civilian population, repeated waves of mass forced displacement in unsafe and inhumane conditions and obstruction of or restrictions on the entry and delivery of life-saving supplies, including humanitarian aid, and essential services in Gaza—all of which occurred simultaneously, for months without respite, compounding each other's harmful effects.

This collection of testimonies is intended as a record of the human toll of the genocide—a way to ensure that neither the violence nor its many victims are forgotten. By also chronicling the devastation inflicted on land, animals, infrastructure, education, and the environment, we aim to show how Israel attacked everything that sustains human life in Palestine.

This project is a collaborative effort across cultures and continents. Our contributors include many established authors we know well and admire, as well as new voices whom we sought out to share their powerful stories. And we are also grateful to the Open Society Foundations for providing us with a generous grant that enabled us to pay our contributors fairly. The two of us are donating our royalties to United Nations Relief and Works Agency for Palestine Refugees in the Near East (UNRWA). UNRWA has been a vital lifeline for 2 million refugees in Gaza, providing essential support such as food, shelter, and healthcare throughout the ongoing genocide. According to UN officials, 269 UNRWA staff members have been killed in Gaza—the highest number of UN personnel lost in any conflict.

Fatima Bhutto and Sonia Faleiro
London, January 2025

# Introduction
## *Mosab Abu Toha*

It's been fifteen months of watching my relatives, friends, students, and teachers massacred, watching the schools where I taught and studied, the farms which I visited with family and friends devastated and genocided by Israel one after the other. Whether or not we reported on each story, the killing machine never failed to find something to finish off.

As someone who has written essays and poems, appeared on TV and radio shows, and given readings and talks in the past few months after surviving the ongoing genocide, I keep asking myself: Why do we write? Why do we share stories? Why do we lend our ears to others' stories?

What if Anne Frank had written her diary and published parts of it in Western magazines and even managed to record and send some stories in her own voice? What if Elie Wiesel and Primo Levi had published *Night* and *Survival in Auschwitz* while still in the concentration camps? What if, what if?

But there is no "what if" here, because so many of us in Palestine, so many of us especially in Gaza have, under the terroristic bombardment, written and published poems and stories, posted videos and photos. Some of these "so many" were killed. They were not killed alone. Some were murdered with a father or a mother, while others were massacred with their wives and kids, some with their parents and siblings, and sometimes with their grandparents, uncles, aunts, and cousins.

My father's cousin, Khader Abu Toha, was killed along with his wife and their seven children and more than eighteen grandchildren.

My dear friend Refaat Alareer was murdered in December 2023 along with his sister Asmaa and his brother Salah and four nephews.

His death was not Refaat's only story. Refaat's "If I Must Die" is a poem he wrote in November 2011, addressed to his daughter Shaimaa—he republished it a few weeks before his murder last year. In April of this year, Israel targeted and killed Shaimaa, her husband, and Refaat's only grandchild— the baby that made Refaat a grandfather—after his murder.

I assure you, Refaat's is not a unique story. Refaat is every one of us. When he said, let it be a tale, he meant it, because his "I" is the collective, the story of every Palestinian, every Gazan. In this heartbreaking poem, the *I* and the *you* are murdered, murdered with family. Refaat, the *I*, died, but the *you*, though Shaimaa was murdered too, becomes each one of us who has read or heard the poem.

When Refaat started his work on *Gaza Writes Back*, which was published in 2014, he decided to compile twenty-two stories to correspond to the number of days Israel terrorized and killed people in Gaza between December 2008 and

January 2009.

Today it's day 426: How many stories do we need to write? How many poems? How many places? How many paintings? How many short movies? How many tears? What can we do to bring life to Gaza?

Gaza was not a city that featured on "best summer travel destinations" lists, though it has strawberry farms, citrus groves, vineyards, and a beach—albeit a beach on a sea unlike any other, with some gunboats six nautical miles off the shore guarding the fish.

Gaza was not even a city for connecting flights on the way to another city on such "best summer travel destinations" lists.

At the age of twenty-seven, my first time leaving Gaza, I started to learn the names of new cities around the world, how far one was from another. Gaza was not listed among them. Not even Yaffa, the original home city of my grandparents.

Gaza is a city where an F-16 drops bombs, where a drone flies not to film a soccer match for distant viewers but only to fire a missile at kids playing soccer on the beach before it fires another at bystanders.

Gaza is a city where bodies, if not already pulverized, remain under the rubble for weeks, a city where souls remain stuck beneath a classroom door, a concrete staircase, or a photo studio wall.

Gaza is a city where a father leaves his shelter to fetch his twins' birth certificates and some juice for a wife recovering from a C-section, only to return and find no wife, no twins, no shelter. A sobbing father holds the certificates in the morgue, certificates that verify the birth of babies, that give names to babies that never set their eyes (no one could tell what color they had been) on the sky or the sun, certificates that prove a father is a father, a mother is a mother—now a father or a mother with no babies. A father holds the certificates, as a student holds their school records and a certificate of distinction, at the door to his parents' house only to find that both of them have died in a car crash at noon.

Gaza is a city whose censored name I've replaced with a strawberry, my favorite fruit that never stopped growing through it all.

Occupation not only censors the land, cutting off water, electricity, medicine, fuel, books, and food, but also the name that refers to life.

Gaza is a city that made her sisters known too: Beit Lahia, Beit Hanoun, Jabalia, Deir al-Balah, Nuseirat, Maghazi, Bureij, az-Zawayda, Khan Younis, and Rafah. People even memorized the names of streets and hospitals. But none of these should be called well-known.

But still Gaza is not a well-known city.

Gaza is not a city.

Gaza is

Gaza

is not.

December 15, 2024
Syracuse, New York

# 1

# On Israeli Settler Colonialism

## Yara Hawari

On January 15, 2025, after over fifteen months of relentless bombardments on the Gaza Strip, a ceasefire between the Israeli regime and Hamas was announced. While a welcome reprieve for the people of Gaza, it did not last long and the devastation caused by Israel's genocidal assault continues to have unimaginable consequences.

At the time of writing, the Palestinian Ministry of Health reported an estimated 53,000 Palestinian fatalities[1]—a toll likely understated, as many bodies remain trapped beneath rubble, unidentified. This figure only reflects those directly killed by Israeli regime airstrikes and artillery. Indirect fatalities, including those resulting from lack of access to medical care, add further to the toll. A *Lancet* report suggests the true number of deaths caused by the genocide may be four times the official count.[2] Hospitals and makeshift

---

1  "Gaza death toll passes 53,000 as Israel drives towards 'conquest,' " *Al Jazeera*, May 16, 2025.
2  Khatib, Rasha et al., "Counting the Dead in Gaza: Difficult but Essential," *Lancet* 404, no. 10449 (July 20, 2024): 237–8.

clinics are overwhelmed by hundreds of thousands of injuries, many life-altering and largely untreated. Gaza now bears the grim distinction of having the largest population of child amputees. Meanwhile, Gaza's infrastructure lies in ruins. Hospitals, schools, sewage systems, and desalination plants are destroyed. The majority of homes have been leveled, displacing families into makeshift tents with limited access to electricity and basic sanitation.

Blinne Ní Ghrálaigh, an adviser to South Africa's legal team which brought the charge of genocide against Israel at the International Court of Justice, remarked in January 2024 that Gaza represents "the first genocide in history where its victims are broadcasting their own destruction in real time, in the desperate, so far vain, hope that the world might do something."[3] Among those documenting the genocide are Palestinian journalists, over 231 of whom have been killed—many reportedly targeted by Israeli drones and bombs while on duty. This toll is double the annual global total of journalist fatalities, yet Western media outlets have largely parroted Israeli regime narratives, offering justifications for the mass slaughter. Meanwhile, a groundswell of grassroots mobilization, particularly on American university campuses, has shown unwavering solidarity with the Palestinian people, and with the people of Gaza in particular, as they endure one of the most brutal assaults on human life in recent history.

Despite widespread public outrage, governments continue

---

3  "World has failed Gaza in 'livestreamed genocide,' South Africa's delegation says at ICJ," video, *Guardian*, accessed November 12, 2024.

to shield the Israeli regime diplomatically and provide material support. The post–World War II vow of "never again" and the subsequent creation of a rules-based international order appear hollow against the political expediency of powerful states. While Western double standards may come as no surprise, the degree to which this genocide has not only been downplayed but also actively facilitated is shocking. The question of "how could this happen" is frequently voiced. Yet it feels naive, particularly when considering the context of entwined forces of imperial interests, white supremacy, and settler colonialism—dynamics that have long provided the Israeli regime with sweeping impunity.

Indeed, understanding the Israeli regime as both a product of Western imperialism and a quasi-US outpost in the Middle East is crucial. This mutually dependent relationship is, in many ways, existential. Israel's survival as a settler-colonial and apartheid state hinges on US material and diplomatic backing; without it, Israel would face profound challenges to its continuity. Likewise, Israel's role is pivotal to American interests in the region, as the US relies on this alliance to uphold its geopolitical influence and sustain its unipolar dominance.[4]

The US may be Israel's foremost ally today, but it was not the first patron of Zionism, the ideological movement behind the establishment of Israel—a moment known as the Nakba, or "catastrophe," by Palestinians. While the US was the first

---

4 Shireen Akram Boshar, "How Israel Became a Watchdog State," in Sumaya Awad and brian bean, eds., *Palestine: A Socialist Introduction* (Chicago: Haymarket Books, 2020).

country to officially recognize Israel, its establishment
unfolded against a backdrop of decades of European colonialism across the region. Following World War I and the
collapse of the Ottoman Empire, European powers vied for
control over the Middle East, with Palestine falling under
British occupation. Viewing Zionism as a means to secure a
lasting presence in the region, Britain aligned itself with the
movement. In 1917, British Foreign Secretary Arthur Balfour
publicly expressed support for "Jewish Zionist aspirations,"
pledging to assist in establishing a "national home for the
Jewish people in Palestine."

The British not only supported the Zionist movement but
actively facilitated Jewish migration to Palestine, protecting
the movement from Palestinian resistance. They enabled the
formation of Zionist militias and infrastructure while
systematically disarming Palestinian groups and undermining Palestinian society. Despite occasional tensions, British
colonialism and the Zionist movement worked hand in
glove—a collaboration that culminated in the mass expulsion of the Indigenous Palestinian population during the
1948 Nakba.[5]

After World War II, the United States turned its attention
to the Middle East as a crucial source of oil and a strategic
bulwark against Soviet expansion. As a newly established
settler state with European roots, Israel quickly emerged as

---

5   For more on the British Mandate period, see Rashid Khalidi, *The
Hundred Years' War on Palestine* (New York: Metropolitan Books, 2020) and
Nur Masalha, *Palestine: A Four Thousand Year History* (London: Zed Books,
2018).

a natural ally. The term "special relationship" between the United States and Israel first gained traction under President Kennedy in the 1960s, when Israel was already a significant recipient of US military aid.[6] The 1967 war solidified Israel's role as a dependable partner capable of countering dissenting Arab regimes. As then-Senator Joe Biden remarked in 1986, "It is the best $3 billion investment we make . . . were there not an Israel, the United States of America would have to invent an Israel to protect her interests in the region." Since Israel's founding over seventy-six years ago, the United States has provided it with more than $310 billion in economic and military aid[7]—$17.9 billion of which was allocated by the Biden administration between October 2023 and October 2024.[8]

The Israeli regime has long portrayed itself as a wall of defense preventing "rampaging hordes from the east" from threatening Western civilization. In a speech to Congress in July 2024, Israeli Prime Minister Benjamin Netanyahu reiterated this stance: "For Iran, Israel is first; America is next. So . . . when we fight Iran . . . we're not only protecting ourselves. We're protecting you." This positioning is neither new nor confined to the Israeli right. The so-called father of

---

6 Shireen Akram Boshar, "How Israel Became a Watchdog State," 32.

7 "US Aid to Israel in Four Charts," Council on Foreign Relations, accessed November 12, 2024.

8 Linda J. Bilmes, William D. Hartung, and Stephen Semler, "United States Spending on Israel's Military Operations and Related US Operations in the Region, October 7, 2023–September 30, 2024," Watson Institute for International and Public Affairs, Brown University, October 7, 2024.

the Zionist movement, Theodor Herzl, wrote in *Der Judenstaat* (1896), "There [in Palestine] we shall be a sector of the wall of Europe against Asia, we shall serve as the outpost of civilization against barbarism."[9]

This idea has been a foundational element of Zionist ideology and remains a key driving force behind US foreign policy in the region. The framing of the Israeli regime as the protector of Western civilization against perceived eastern threats continues to shape both Israeli strategic goals and American support for its actions, ensuring the continuation of a deeply intertwined relationship between the two regimes.

Such a notion is, of course, rooted in a belief in white supremacy, which elevates white civilization and peoples as superior while categorizing others as inherently barbaric or violent. Although many Western governments and institutions attempt to mask this ideology with a veneer of liberalism, it often resurfaces. In 2022, EU Foreign Affairs and Security Policy Chief Josep Borrell described Europe as "a garden"—a model of political freedom, economic prosperity, and social cohesion—while likening the rest of the world to a "jungle," implying that it was a violent, disorderly place that could threaten the order of the garden. Borrell apologized following backlash, but he later reaffirmed the garden-versus-jungle metaphor.[10]

---

9    Theodore Herzl, *Der Judenstaat*, 1896.
10   Jorge Liboreiro, "Josep Borell Apologises for Controversial Garden vs Jungle Metaphor but Defends Speech," *Euronews*, October 19, 2022.

Israeli Prime Minister Netanyahu invoked a similar image at the onset of the genocide in Gaza, framing Israel's assault as "a struggle between the children of light and the children of darkness, between humanity and the law of the jungle."[11] This deeply racist language reinforces a worldview that dehumanizes the Global South and upholds the idea of its inferiority.

For the Israeli regime, a settler-colonial project, Palestinians are not only regarded as inferior and "children of darkness," but as a people that must be displaced, if not eliminated. This mindset was evident even in the early stages of the Zionist project. In 1937, David Ben-Gurion wrote to his son, stating: "We [the Zionist settlers] must expel the Arabs and take their place," shortly after the British Peel Commission proposed partitioning the land into two states. This historical context underscores that what is happening in Gaza and Palestine today is not an aberration but a continuation of a project that began over a century ago.

It is crucial, therefore, to avoid exceptionalizing the Israeli regime. Settler-colonial entities worldwide—including the US and Australia—have committed genocide to erase Indigenous populations and secure the continuation of their colonial projects. What is unfolding in Palestine is not an isolated event but part of a broader, global history of violent, dispossessive tactics aimed at eliminating Indigenous peoples and solidifying settler control over land.

---

11   Benjamin Netanyahu, excerpt from opening remarks of the Knesset Winter Assembly, October 16, 2023.

In late December 2023, South Africa brought charges of genocide against the Israeli regime before the International Court of Justice (ICJ). A key component of the case focused on genocidal intent, backed by numerous public statements made by Israeli politicians and officials. For instance, in October 2023, Israeli Minister of Defense Yoav Gallant told Israeli troops entering Gaza, "Gaza won't return to what it was before . . . we will eliminate everything."[12] A month later, the ICJ concluded that "plausible acts of genocide" were being committed. This ruling echoed what Palestinians and many within the international human rights community had been asserting for months. The ICJ subsequently ordered the Israeli regime to take all necessary measures to prevent actions in contravention of the UN genocide convention. In November 2024, a UN special committee also stated that Israeli regime actions in Gaza are "consistent with the characteristics of genocide." Unsurprisingly, Israel failed to comply with the ICJ's demands, instead launching a delegitimization campaign against the court and other international institutions.

The Israeli regime's response fits into a long-standing pattern in which international legal rulings and findings are totally ignored. As Francesca Albanese, the United Nations Special Rapporteur on the Occupied Palestinian Territories, has pointed out, while every state commits international law violations, the Israeli regime stands out for its continuous unlawful occupation, disregard for hundreds of UN

---

12   "Gaza won't return to what it was before. We will eliminate everything." Video, *Al Arabiya* (English), October 11, 2023.

resolutions, and violation of international humanitarian law, human rights law, the apartheid convention, and the genocide convention. Israel has also been relentless in its attacks on UN facilities and staff, further demonstrating its disregard for international legal norms.

Despite all this, the Israeli regime continues to enjoy diplomatic and material support from countries around the world. It is not the pariah state it should be, nor has it faced meaningful sanctions or repercussions for its ongoing assault on the Palestinian people. This impunity is unparalleled, and it is precisely this unaccountability that made the genocide in Gaza not just foreseeable, but inevitable. The absence of meaningful international action to hold Israel accountable for its violations—compounded by the unwavering support from powerful global actors—has facilitated an environment in which such atrocities can occur without significant consequence.

What is abundantly clear is that this cycle of impunity will not be broken by the institutions that have allowed it to flourish. Palestinians have known this for a long time, and many in the world are also beginning to understand this. Disruption of this reality and the status quo require seismic shifts in global politics—a feat that may seem overwhelming but one that also positions the many against the few.

# 2

# Hamas Contained: A History of Palestinian Resistance

## *Tareq Baconi*

Israel managed to divide and rule the Palestinians by creating two enclaves, or Bantustan-like structures, where Palestinian parties governed without enjoying any real sovereignty, operating under the unyielding structure of Israeli rule.

I make a key distinction, however, between the West Bank and the Gaza Strip. Rule in the former was compliant; the Palestinian Authority had committed to security co-ordination, recognized the State of Israel, and cracked down on resistance. Under the guise of the "peace process," liberation was demoted in favor of governance, turning the Palestinian Authority into a central pillar of Israeli apartheid.

Rule in the latter, by contrast, was grounded in resistance, whereby Hamas had turned the body of the Palestinian Authority, which it had been elected to in 2006 and from which it governed Gaza after its takeover in 2007, into a structure from which to challenge Israeli rule. Between 2007 and 2023, Israel relied primarily on Hamas to govern Gaza's population, obfuscating its own legal responsibility as the

occupying power while adopting a "mowing the lawn" policy
to deter Hamas militarily. For Israel, this dynamic worked so
well that it never developed a political strategy for Gaza,
pursuing—as it did in the West Bank—measures to manage,
rather than resolve, the occupation.

The shocking Hamas-led attack on October 7, 2023,
undermined a number of these assumptions and was a turning point in the Palestinian struggle for liberation. The
offensive was named "Operation al-Aqsa Flood" in Arabic, a
title that reaffirmed Hamas's use of al-Aqsa as a Palestinian,
Arab, and Islamic symbol speaking far beyond the confines of
Palestine. Hamas fighters converged on Israeli territory by
sea, air, and ground under the cover of rockets fired from
Gaza. Many of the fighters who pushed into Israeli towns
were descendants of refugees from the very lands they glided
into, stepping onto those grounds for the first time since their
families' expulsion. Within hours they had besieged the
towns; broken into homes; killed 695 Israeli civilians, 373
soldiers and policemen, and 71 foreigners—mostly Thai
workers—and kidnapped 240 others to use for negotiating
the release of thousands of imprisoned Palestinians.

With the benefit of hindsight, it is clear that Hamas's
containment was finite, lasting for sixteen years between 2007
and 2023. At its core, Hamas's attack was an unprecedented
and bloody display of anti-colonial violence. It can be read
only as a response to Israel's relentless provocation of occupying another people, besieging them, and denying their
freedom and right to self-determination for more than
seventy-five years. So thoroughly was Gaza erased from the

Israeli psyche that Hamas's offensive came as if out of nowhere, dealing the most lethal blow to the Israeli military and public since 1948. Within hours, the infrastructure that had been put in place to contain Hamas, and with it to wish away the Palestinians of Gaza, was trampled before our disbelieving eyes. As Palestinian fighters and civilians burst into Israel, the collision between the myth of Israel as a Jewish and democratic state without responsibility for its non-Jewish subjects and its reality as a purveyor of violent apartheid was shocking, tragic, and ultimately irreversible.

By breaking out of its prison, Hamas revealed the strategic poverty at the heart of the assumption that Palestinians would acquiesce indefinitely to their imprisonment, that Israel could maintain—and expand—its colonial regime at no cost to Israeli society. The movement broke through a central pillar of Zionism, that Israel would be able to provide a safe haven for Jews without having to address the Palestinian question in political terms. And in so doing, it laid to waste the viability of Israel's partitionist approach, that Palestinians can be siphoned off into Bantustans while the state that controls their territories continues to enjoy peace and security.

In that sense, October 7 ushered in a paradigmatic rupture, hurtling Palestinians and Israelis from an era that had lasted more than seventy-five years into a new reality, the contours of which remain unknown at the time of this writing. The rupture risks drawing the region into an all-out conflagration, encompassing Iran, Lebanon, Jordan, Egypt, Syria, Iraq, and Yemen. Rather than attempt to de-escalate, the administration of President Joseph R. Biden poured fuel on a raging fire, likening Hamas's offensive to the al-Qaeda attacks of 9/11, a thinly disguised attempt to preemptively excuse Israel's extreme use of force in Gaza.

Under the guise of self-defense, and with an American green light, Israel retaliated with the stated goal of decimating Hamas. The extent of Israel's killing and destruction in the Gaza Strip has prompted scholars, experts, and lawyers to argue that the Israeli state is committing genocide against Palestinians. At the time of this writing, more than 53,000 Palestinians have been killed, most of them civilians. The UN has called Gaza a "graveyard for children," given the thousands murdered by Israeli forces, who sought to obliterate all signs of life in the strip—destroying schools, hospitals, bakeries, and universities. In response to Western complicity in Israel's violence, in December 2023 South Africa brought charges of genocide against Israel at the International Court of Justice, prompting a ruling from the court that such accusations were "plausible" and ordering provisional measures to be taken by Israel to minimize the killing of civilians, all of which were ignored. In January 2024, a California federal district court also ruled that a plausible case of genocide could be brought against the Biden administration for abetting this crime.

Some analysts have described Hamas's move as suicidal, given Israel's reaction, or irresponsible, given the enormous death toll it has led to among Palestinians. Whether either of these characterizations is accurate depends on an analysis of what options Hamas had. There is no doubt that the attack itself was a decisive rupture. From a perspective strictly of military strategy, Hamas certainly had the option of sustaining its equilibrium with Israel indefinitely, remaining constricted within the framework of the blockade. With the release of its 2017 revised charter, Hamas had explored options for further political engagement, formalizing many of the positions described in this book, including accepting a Palestinian state on the 1967 line. There was very little Israeli, let alone international, interest in questioning the blockade, even when mobilization against it took the form of popular protests, such as in the Great March of Return— and no effort at all to respond to these changes in Hamas's position. Many Palestinians in Gaza came to describe their confinement as a slow death, and Israeli, regional, and international actors assumed that Palestinians had been defeated, unable to fundamentally overturn the structure of Israeli apartheid.

Seen in this light, it is Hamas's acquiescence to Israeli rule that might be considered suicidal. That Hamas opted to disrupt this dominating structure suggests that it was behaving strategically and remains dedicated to the belief that it is playing a long game. The movement irreversibly shattered the false sense of security Israelis had cloaked themselves in and their failed efforts to present Israel as invincible and impenetrable. The evident weakness and fragility of Israel's military can be exploited in the future through a reconstituted Hamas or through another military formation equally committed to armed resistance as a means of liberation. In other words, the disruption itself has emerged as a space for alternative possibilities to surface, whereas, prior to that, there was only the calcified certainty of continued Palestinian oppression.

This is precisely what is existential for Israel, and, supported by Western allies, the state believes that the only way to survive this blow is through the decimation of Hamas, to rebuild deterrence so that nothing like Operation al-Aqsa Flood can happen again. Prime Minister Benjamin Netanyahu has called for a "total victory," insisting that Hamas will be dismantled, while Defense Minister Yoav Gallant has said that Israel will "wipe Hamas off the face of this world." Israel will fail—and is already failing—in attaining this objective. As in any asymmetric struggle, the guerrilla fighters merely have to avoid losing to emerge victorious, whereas the conventional army will lose if it does not achieve its over-arching goals. And the goal of decimating Hamas as a movement is as vague as it is unachievable.

Such a strategic and military reading of Hamas's calculus is almost entirely absent from current Western analysis of the movement and its rationale in the wake of October 7. The dehumanization of Palestinians is so thoroughly pervasive and so unquestioningly echoed by Western leaders that any effort to challenge Israel's system of domination is met with perplexed reactions and uniform condemnation. In this reading, Hamas acted irrationally, Palestinians in Gaza were disposable to the movement as veritable human shields, and the system in its whole was sustainable. These reactions cohere with a broader tendency toward Western hypocrisy and racism, which has normalized the occupation and daily killing of Palestinians, and reacted only when the violence is directed at Israeli Jews. It is a reading that removes all agency from Palestinian actors seeking to overturn a regime bent on their erasure. It is also one that fails to grapple with the violence and complex ethics of anti-colonial resistance, painting all forms of mobilization by Palestinians—peaceful or otherwise—as unacceptable.

Still, Hamas's operation and the ongoing genocide have raised significant questions for Palestinians, regarding Hamas, Gaza, and the future of their struggle. Many Palestinians, for instance, have voiced worries that Hamas's offensive is the beginning of another existential crisis. The looming possibility of ethnic cleansing must not be underplayed, and the staggering death toll that civilians in Gaza are experiencing must give collective pause to reflect on the enormous cost that Hamas's attack instigated, even as the main responsibility for this violence sits with Israel's regime of apartheid. Furthermore, the wholesale destruction of Gaza has all but made this tiny sliver of land uninhabitable, so that even if the genocide stops, there is a longer-term question as to whether Palestinian life can be sustained there. With the knowledge that Hamas and other factions have gathered over the years, and the expectation that the movement's offensive would unleash fury on Palestinians, many argue that Hamas should have been prepared for this violence and planned accordingly. Yes, the thinking goes, Hamas's offensive was strategic in its disruption of the structure of apartheid, but to what end? Where do Palestinians go from here? Determining whether Hamas's calculus paid off, despite this tragic loss of life, is something Palestinians will be debating for years to come.

What is also worth debating is whether Hamas's leaders had anticipated that the operation would unfold the way it did.

This attack was planned and executed by the military wing in Gaza under the leadership of Yahya Sinwar with such a degree of secrecy that it took most of Hamas's political leaders by surprise. It raises real questions as to how Hamas as an organization has evolved—and will continue to evolve—from here, given that such a transformative operation was carried out primarily by the military wing, with the political bureau being forced to play catch-up.

Apart from the strict military objectives, Hamas had other factors underpinning its calculus in planning this operation, most notably its ambivalence toward governance. Hamas was shackled by its role as a governing authority in Gaza. When the party ran for elections in 2006, it harbored great reservations about taking on a governing role or even participating in the Palestinian Authority. Hamas leaders articulated that rather than accepting the limitations of governance under occupation, as Fatah had done through the Palestinian Authority in the West Bank, the movement was intent on using its election victory to revolutionize the political establishment. Hamas spoke about the need to build a "society of resistance, an economy of resistance, an ideology of resistance," through those very structures—and to use this as a stepping stone into the PLO, from which it could lead alongside other political factions to create a vision for the liberation of Palestine and for representing Palestinians in their entirety, beyond those in the occupied territories.

With no real hopes for statehood, Hamas understood that a focus on governance and administration meant beautifying a Bantustan within Israel's apartheid system and having few prospects for sovereignty. That is indeed the model in the West Bank, and it would have taken on a more extreme character in the Gaza Strip.

October 7 has clearly shown that the movement had been using this time precisely to revolutionize its base, as had always been its intention. It is not inevitable that Hamas's strategic shift and its successful disruption of Israeli apartheid will lead to Palestinian liberation. It is now up to Palestinians primarily, as well as other regional and international actors, to use this moment of disequilibrium to pursue a more just future in Palestine and Israel. What is certain is that there is no return to what existed before. Yet this is precisely what Israeli, US, and other Western leaders and diplomats are preparing for. Even before Israel's genocidal violence has subsided, the discussion has turned to the day after.

All indications point to a US-Israeli decision to try to replicate in the Gaza Strip the—in their view—successful model of Palestinian collaborationist rule that exists in the West Bank. Rather than engaging in an inclusive political process, accounting for Hamas and other factions, and allowing Palestinians to choose their own representative leaders, Israel and the United States are replaying an age-old approach of choosing compliant leaders who can do the bidding of external powers. This is being pursued under the banner of supposedly unifying the Palestinian territories, after destroying Hamas, with both parties conveniently erasing their own complicity in facilitating this disunity until now. The goal for both is not reunification but the pursuit of acquiescent rule: the creation of a governing structure in which a pliant leadership administers civil needs under an overarching configuration of Israeli domination.

To facilitate the installation of an authority chosen by Israel and the United States requires nothing less than razing Gaza and killing or displacing its inhabitants—the genocide now unfolding.

Hamas's military infrastructure will have been dealt a blow by the time the genocide ends, although not one as severe as the Israeli establishment and Western powers claim. The movement has prevailed on the battlefield without succumbing to any of the military goals that Israel has sought. After more than six months of relentless bombardment, the only release of Israeli captives occurred almost exclusively through diplomatic negotiations. The vast tunnel infrastructure that Hamas built, which will be studied for decades to come as an innovative site of asymmetric anti-colonial struggle, has withstood the ferocious assault and offered protection to most of Hamas's fighting arsenal. The movement might yet be expelled from Gaza; its fighters might yet be hunted down and killed; its leaders might yet be pursued abroad; the military wing might yet disintegrate and regroup as a decentralized network of cells operating throughout the Gaza Strip, and therefore under a different form of organizational structure in relation to the political bureau; Hamas might yet reemerge in the West Bank, where it enjoys popularity and has a vast network of support.

It is impossible to predict the exact outcome, but what is clear is that Hamas's political ideology—its commitment to and belief in armed struggle against colonial violence—will persist. Palestinian resistance is cyclical. Parties emerge that defy Israeli colonization, and, opposed by excessive military force and diplomatic marginalization, they are compelled to acquiesce and retreat. It is too early to tell how Hamas will emerge from this moment, but that resistance will remain cyclical is assured. There is a continuum of Palestinian political demands that stretch back to 1948 and well before Israel's establishment. Whether Hamas survives in its current incarnation is a red herring: Palestinian resistance against Israeli apartheid, armed and otherwise, will persist as long as apartheid persists, and as long as Palestinians are not annihilated as a people.

The form of this defiance is contingent on how Israel will deal with the Gaza Strip itself, and how successful it will be at exterminating or expelling the Palestinians there. Early signs indicate that Israel is experimenting with ways to reinstate some version of the Village Leagues, whereby Israel's occupying forces engage with local leaders who can administer the population—the model often invoked by right-wing leaders seeking to do away with the Palestinian Authority. This model might be pursued either as a longer-term structure, whereby Israel's military reoccupies and resettles the

Gaza Strip, carving it up into distinct silos (much like the Oslo Accords' Areas A, B, and C in the West Bank), or as a shorter-term configuration, until the administration of the Palestinian Authority can be brought back into Gaza, where it will be expected to govern as it does in the West Bank. Such an entity will have even less legitimacy than it does today, which is hard to imagine. Yet it is this model, that of reunifying the West Bank and Gaza under the rule of the Palestinian Authority, without challenging Israel's domination, that the international community touts under the banner of the "two-state solution." It is a framework that allows for Palestinian autonomy short of sovereignty and is nothing more than the repackaging of apartheid in a more palatable guise.

However these efforts pan out, it is clear that Hamas will no longer exist as a governing authority and will revert to its role as being primarily a military wing, albeit one that is weakened, operating outside the internationally recognized institutions of Palestinian liberation. From its perspective, the movement is seeking to leverage the rupture it instigated on October 7 to reinvigorate the Palestinian struggle for liberation—to build political unity among the various factions, whether in the body of a reunified Palestinian Authority that breaks from the tenets of the Oslo Accords or in the framework of the PLO, and to revive that structure in a more inclusive and representative manner. Since October 7, Hamas has articulated its political demands, calling for its readiness to accept the formation of a Palestinian state with East Jerusalem as its capital, and for holding Israel accountable. These calls have been disregarded, as Western powers extend a cloak of protection to Israel to pursue its goal of destroying Hamas and the Gaza Strip, enabling it to continue dealing with the Palestinian struggle for self-determination through military, rather than political, means.

Hamas's military operation might not have been accompanied by sufficient strategic planning to meet the immensity of this moment, and its political aims might ultimately fall short. Yet to place the future of Palestinian liberation solely on the movement's shoulders is also short-sighted. It is true that Hamas is the only major Palestinian organization that is militarily active, but it is one faction of a much broader and more diverse ecosystem of Palestinian organizations, factions, and institutions that are mobilizing around this moment to challenge Israel's apartheid and to push back against a return to October 6, which is the clear aim of Israel and members of the international community. Two lessons can be garnered from October 7: that Israel's apartheid is not invincible, and that however the "day after" is packaged, it will fail unless Palestinians secure their inalienable right to self-determination as a people. Israeli political leaders and their subcontractor parties in the Palestinian Authority have yet to heed this lesson. But grassroots organizers, Hamas's allies, and other political and military formations have. Whatever emerges from this moment, and however Hamas's next chapter will be written, it is clear that the movement has successfully shattered the delusion that Israeli apartheid can persist at no cost.

The vast destruction of the Gaza Strip and the horrifying loss of civilian life are a painful blow to Palestinians, reminiscent of the Nakba of 1948. Yet, simultaneously, Palestine is back on the top of the global agenda—with growing recognition that it must be addressed, even if the events of October 7 have polarized debate. Moreover, Palestine is now being discussed not through the deadening policy language of state-building and partition, but rather through its first principles, as the facade of the peace process has given way to an understanding of the reality of Israeli apartheid and its rejection of life in Palestine. While it is Hamas that ushered in this new phase and broke from the ossified reality that existed in the preceding decades, it is up to Palestinians writ large to shape the future trajectory of their struggle.

There is one final point that must be stated with certainty. The fate of Palestine is not only about Palestine, but about the global order and the struggle for a just world in which this topic is contested at an institutional level. The duplicity of Western powers in leveraging global institutions like the UN to further their own hegemonic projects is no longer deniable, particularly when the Western reactions to Russia's invasion of Ukraine are compared with the reactions to Israel's genocide of the Palestinians in Gaza. Countries like South Africa have taken note, challenging Western hegemony at the International Court of Justice, by bringing the case of this genocide to international forums. This is but one example of how the Global South is pushing for an end to American unipolarity and Western hegemony, which have historically enabled and supported the Zionist colonization of Palestine, and mobilizing for a more just, equitable, and decolonial world order. The unprecedented global mobilization against

Israel's genocide affirms that Gaza is a pivot. Drawing on the words of the Francophone Martinique poet, author, and politician Aimé Césaire, it is through Gaza that the "colonial boomerang" is ricocheting back to the metropole.

# 3
# I Grant You Refuge

*Hiba Abu Nada, translated by
Huda J. Fakhreddine*

*1.*

I grant you refuge
in invocation and prayer.
I bless the neighborhood and the minaret
to guard them
from the rocket
from the moment
it is a general's command
until it becomes
a raid.
I grant you and the little ones refuge,
the little ones who
change the rocket's course
before it lands
with their smiles.

*2.*

I grant you and the little ones refuge,
the little ones now asleep like chicks in a nest.
They don't walk in their sleep toward dreams.
They know death lurks outside the house.
Their mothers' tears are now doves
following them, trailing behind
every coffin.

*3.*

I grant the father refuge,
the little ones' father who holds the house upright
when it tilts after the bombs.
He implores the moment of death:
"Have mercy. Spare me a little while.
For their sake, I've learned to love my life.
Grant them a death
as beautiful as they are."

*4.*

I grant you refuge
from hurt and death,
refuge in the glory of our siege,
here in the belly of the whale.
Our streets exalt God with every bomb.
They pray for the mosques and the houses.

And every time the bombing begins in the North,
our supplications rise in the South.


5.


I grant you refuge
from hurt and suffering.
With words of sacred scripture
I shield the oranges from the sting of phosphorous
and the shades of cloud from the smog.
I grant you refuge in knowing
that the dust will clear,
and they who fell in love and died together
will one day laugh.

*Poet, novelist, and educator Hiba Abu Nada was killed by an Israeli airstrike on her home in Khan Younis, Gaza, on October 20, 2023. She was thiry-two.*

# 4

## The Feeds of the IDF Depict What Zionism Can't See

### *Mary Turfah*

*What is wrong with the Israelis?* The question as I have heard it asked, with emphasis on the word *wrong*, is raised not in response to footage of the genocidal death and destruction the IDF has wrought upon Gaza, but to what crumbs Israeli soldiers themselves have shared of it. A small sampling of the genre, organized alphabetically by mood:

**Carefree** An Israeli soldier inflates a soccer ball, saying to the camera—and presumably his child—"Before we went into Gaza, I promised you that we would bounce a ball on the beach . . . I took a ball [I've] carried around." Another soldier asks him if he'd brought the pump with him, too, and he says, "Of course, what do you think, I bought it here in Gaza?" Once the ball is ready the soldiers kick it around in a circle, three of them wearing swim trunks they'd possibly found in the drawers of the bedroom of the people whose house they're inside. Someone walks the phone recording all of this through a large hole in the wall and, showing us the ruins of Gaza, says, "What a view! What a beach!"

**(Casually) Destructive** A bit of a misnomer, since they're all destructive. I mean actively destroying things. In one video, two Israeli soldiers lean against a ledge. One lights a cigarette as the entire backdrop explodes.

**Devoted/Birthday** A soldier blows up a residential block to celebrate his daughter's birthday.

**Domestic** Israeli soldiers show off their cooking skills in the homes of people they've killed or displaced (or both). There is olive oil in every house, they say. "The Gazan cuisine, from what we saw, is full of spices."

**Graffiti artist** A soldier poses next to what I presume is his work—the words, "Instead of erasing graffiti, let us erase Gaza," spray-painted in fire-truck red onto a building in Gaza. Beneath the show of unifying genocidal intent, he has added the Star of David, also in red.

**Feminist** A female IDF soldier walks alongside a row of Palestinian men raising their arms in surrender, identification papers in hand. (The *New York Times* wrote, "Israel's female combat soldiers are pushing new boundaries after rushing into battle," in an admiring report on women's participation in the war. "Israeli Women Fight on Front Line in Gaza, a First," January 19, 2024.)

**Looter (Thrifty)** Israeli soldiers carry large sums of cash and jewelry, taken from homes in Gaza. A soldier holds a delicate silver chain between his fingers; another soldier, recording him, says, "Noa, look, your boyfriend brought you a new necklace." He pauses, then adds, "Made in Gaza."

**Predatory** In one photo, two Israeli soldiers snuggle up in the twin-size bed of a child they've either killed or displaced. In another, a child's doll is splayed out on the hood of a car. Another soldier in a child's bed. And another. Maybe this one goes in *carefree*: soldiers giggle uncontrollably in an emptied playground, pushing each other in red-binned carts.

**Romantic** An Israeli soldier has announced his upcoming wedding date onto an inside wall of a house belonging to people Israel had either killed or displaced (or both).

**Vulgar/Kinky** In one photo, two soldiers walk through the streets of Gaza. The soldier on the left wears a nude bra over his uniform. The soldier on the right holds the tip of the cup between his fingers. His tongue is out. In another video, a soldier dangles women's underwear over the face of a colleague, asleep on a couch inside a Palestinian home. In a video, a soldier shares a revelation: "I'm going through these terrorists' houses looking for guns and explosives . . . at every single house"—he can hardly contain his excitement—"inside of Gaza this is what I see. Every single—unbelievable." He opens a dresser, narrating, "Two or three drawers stuffed with the most, ehh, exotic lingerie that you can imagine. Just piles of it. Every single house. Stuffed to the brim! Look at that!" he says, dipping in a hand, lacing his fingers through it, "Unbelieeevaboh," his British accent thickening. He adds, following a strange grunting sound, "These naughty, naughty Gazans." The video, shared as an Instagram story, includes a poll: the prompt is *what dya think?*," and viewers choose from the following: 1. Kinky terrorism, 2. Wtf?, 3. Halal, 4. Haram.

I'm sure I've missed some all-timers.

While many viewers might find this content disturbing, *they* are not the target audience. In Israel, where a majority opposes a ceasefire and supports starving Gaza, this content is, on the whole, well-received. It offers the folks back home an image of fortified dominance, the illusion of control. In March 2024, the liberal Zionist daily *Haaretz* detailed, in a report titled "We're Not Only Here to Fuck Hamas," how battlefield imagery has flooded online dating profiles in Israel. Beyond its sexual currency, this content, like the torture of Palestinians aired on mainstream Israeli television, functions as entertainment. Telegram channels sharing graphic images of dead or dying Palestinians—and foreign aid workers— have amassed hundreds of thousands of subscribers. The image of the shrunken corpse of a nine-year-old Palestinian boy with cerebral palsy, starved to death by Israel, appeared on one feed as part of a mock–movie poster that included the boy's severely cachectic face alongside a picture of E.T. in his bicycle basket, riding into the night sky. The film would be called *A.H.M.E.T.* The boy's actual name was Yazan; his mother called him Yazouna.

A parallel, seemingly contradictory trend among Israelis is the widespread dismissal of these atrocities—the dead bodies, the grieving siblings, the starving children—as fake, part of what Zionists call "Pallywood," Palestinians' conspiratorial manipulation of the worldwide media to demonize Israel. A grandfather mourning his five-month-old grandson, killed by Israel in Gaza, was accused in the *Jerusalem Post* of crying over a doll. The *Post* later retracted the story, "Al Jazeera Posts Blurred Doll, Claims It to Be a Dead Palestinian Baby," after it had gone viral.

The pervasive sadism cannot be explained away as the behavior of soldiers at war, adapted to the needs of a new generation whose social media addiction compels them to document their cruelty. The tendencies to revel and deny coexist, not just within the population but within the same person. Near the border with Egypt, a settler, there to block humanitarian aid from entering Gaza, tells a journalist that (a) the Palestinians are not starving, and (b) they will continue to receive no food (that is, starve) until the hostages are released.

These justifications are not for him; he throws them at a wall, and the listener is free to see what sticks.

People ask *what's wrong with the Israelis* because, I suspect, they find the depravity difficult to believe, let alone comprehend. Attempts to ascribe motive are met with visceral revulsion, an affront to something fundamental and big, like

morality. I wonder how a person gets here. And I know our
responsibility is not to find a way to psychologically accommodate it, but rather to work to stop it. Still, with every snuff
video I find myself back at that same question. In strictly
political terms I can appreciate the clarity it allows. Watching
these soldiers, I do not feel concern, or anything at all, for
*them*. Instead, the feeling is that of looking at a person, and
where you expect recognition you find its inverse—a stunned
alienation.

The cruelty itself, on display in videos, like the one taken
from the vantage point of Israeli soldiers driving their tank
over the I LOVE GAZA sign (that greets visitors entering Gaza
through the Rafah crossing), is somehow less disturbing than
that it is presented with naked glee—no trace of the sober air
that marks a person "doing what needs to be done" or an
awareness that the rest of the world might not receive overt,
genocidal sadism as welcomingly as the average Israeli. It's
like they can't see us seeing them. Or maybe they don't care.
Attempts to explain Israeli behavior often reach for the
biomedical. *Surely this cannot be willed*, they think, and so it
must be pathological. In medicine, when a patient is unable to
grasp their condition—as when a person experiencing hallucinations does not recognize them as such—we say they lack
insight. Because we encounter the Israelis' smug cruelty most
acutely through individuals—be they government officials,
soldiers, or formerly-known-as-Twitter warriors—it is easy
to perceive it as an individuated "settler psychosis." Psychosis
replaces politics and history; it obscures how societies arrive
at ideologies, reinforce and transmit them over time; and how

dehumanization is preceded, constructed, and justified, so that it can be rendered with intention.

A Hebrew-only article in *Haaretz*'s food section from February 2024 interviewed two Israeli soldiers about their culinary habits in Gaza. Among the questions posed was a delicately worded consideration of the fact that these homes did not belong to them. "Can you tell us a little about the feelings of cooking and eating in the home of a Gazan family knowing that they had to evacuate or flee?" the interviewer asked, omitting the obvious third possibility. One soldier opened his reply with nonspecific remorse, "There are mixed feelings, no doubt. After all, I use their tools, in their house, when they are not here. *But*," he pivoted, "on the other hand, we have to eat . . . It is important to clarify that these are abandoned houses, some of them destroyed or destined for demolition, and this is the way the IDF fights in Gaza." On the one hand, there is the awareness of a world beyond them. On the other, the necessity of survival. Before and after, the logic of elimination.

Palestinians have been "abandoning" their houses for a long time. At the start of the Nakba in 1948, a member of the kibbutz called Karmia—between Ashkelon and Gaza, built over the Palestinian village of Hiribya—wrote of settling there in the 1950s, "I did not feel like I was stealing from others, I did not feel any guilt at all . . . those who had lived in the kibbutz area had abandoned their homes and fled." This is what the kibbutz members had been told. In fact, Hiribya had been targeted by Israeli air raids during

Operation Yo'av; its survivors fled south. The operation was carried out following a series of United Nations Security Council Resolutions (UNSCR) calling for a ceasefire between Israel and the Arabs, and after the assassination of the UN mediator, Count Folke Bernadotte (the "first UN casualty"). Bernadotte had arranged a truce and insisted Israel present a plan to ensure the safe return of Palestinian refugees to their homes, thus laying the groundwork for UNRWA. His assassination was carried out by members of the Stern Gang (a Zionist terrorist group later absorbed into the Israeli Defense Forces) whose actions Israel—also condemned by the UN Security Council (in Resolution 59)—refused to investigate.

It was a time of euphemisms. At a high-level meeting in August 1948, Ben-Gurion and several of his officials discussed the "problem" of Palestinian refugees, and how to prevent their return. Various options were presented: the destruction of villages or their timely resettlement with Jewish settlers. The next day, in a separate meeting, the cultivation of fields on "abandoned" lands was discussed. At least one person at the first meeting expressed "reservations about settling Jews in Arab houses." Attendance had been curated to minimize such positions: members of Mapam, a leftist Zionist party that envisioned the inclusion of Arabs in their state, were excluded for their "departure from reality and their ideological hallucinations." Note the language of psychosis to describe an unwillingness to accept the obvious. Russian Zionist Ze'ev Jabotinsky in his 1923 essay "The Iron Wall" asked readers to "consider all the precedents with which they are acquainted, and see whether there is one solitary instance of any colonisation being carried on with the consent of the native population." He then answered his own question: "There is no such precedent."

The justification behind implementation of the population "transfer" was that war suspends morality. In February 1948, addressing the consciences and practical concerns of those who worried how the Zionists could build a state, when they owned around 6 percent of the land, Ben-Gurion reasoned, "the war will give us the land. The concepts of 'ours' and 'not ours' are peace concepts, only, and in war they lose their whole meaning."

To sustain the Zionist project, the Machiavellian clarity common among Zionist leadership required ideological integration into the population. Among the more idealist kibbutzim members who had arrived to cultivate the land in the 1940s and construct a socialist utopia, some struggled to reconcile their politics with the reality they were recruited to establish. My grandfather's village, Salha (spelled *Saliha* by the British and their colonial inheritors), was settled in 1949, soon after it had been ethnically cleansed through a massacre that killed an eleventh of its inhabitants and drove the rest to Lebanon, after which they were barred return and shot at if they attempted to. Part of the land was renamed Avivim; the rest, Yi'ron. A member of kibbutz Yi'ron wrote in the second issue of their newsletter:

> The facts are that men, women, old people and babies were murdered, villages were destroyed and burned, without justification . . . There will only be atonement

when those guilty of murder will be judged and when the houses and lands of the people of Saliha will be returned to them . . . but who but us, sitting upon skulls and ruins and eating from the "abandoned land," who but us knows that none of this will ever come to pass? . . . What a horrific contradiction! We, who "uphold brotherhood of nations and faith in man," will we be silent and will try to find atonement for that great crime, in ourselves?

While this moral dilemma was by no means common—none of the issues he raised were revisited in subsequent newsletters—that it was raised at all suggests the settlers knew. *Of course* they knew. Palestinians have spent a long time asking how Zionists could live with themselves. In Palestinian writer and militant Ghassan Kanafani's novella *Returning to Haifa*, the Palestinian protagonist Said and his wife, seizing on the opportunity of transiently ruptured borders following the 1967 war, return to their home, "abandoned" in 1948. They knock, and a stranger, an old woman, opens the door. "May we come in?" they ask, and the old woman steps aside, allowing them to enter

with slow, hesitant steps. They began to pick out the things around them with a certain bewilderment. The entrance seemed smaller . . . [Said] looked around, rediscovering the items sometimes little by little and sometimes all at once, like someone recovering from a long period of unconsciousness . . . The old woman was sitting in front of them on the arm of one of the chairs, looking at them with a blank smile on her face. Finally, without changing her smile, she said, "I have been expecting you for a long time." . . . Said leaned forward and asked her: "Do you know who we are?" She nodded several times to emphasize her certainty. She thought for a moment, choosing her words, then said slowly: "You are the owners of this house. [I know] from everything. From the photographs, from the way the two of you stood in front of the door."

It is the perspective of Kanafani's protagonist, the Palestinian, that the settler at the kibbutz built atop Salha decided to accommodate. He looked around him and thought of the people, the lives destroyed "without justification" whose echoes were everywhere, in everything, and understood there should be consequences. I'm unsure whether he left or stayed. The home was eventually destroyed.

In the decades before the Nakba, the justifications for colonizing Palestine had been the decision itself. God and the British—in the Balfour Declaration of 1917—had promised them the land, and it was their duty to actualize it. The Palestinians, whom Zionists still refer to as "Arabs" (a linguistic distancing of the people from the land), were in the way. "My great-grandfather," writes Ari Shavit in *My Promised Land*, about his ancestor's decision to settle in Palestine in 1897, "does not see because he is motivated by the need not to see. He does not see because if he does see, he will have to turn back."

In those early days, before the state's machinery had refined the process, the Zionist project's foot soldiers sometimes struggled to sustain the narrative they imposed onto reality. Israeli historian Ilan Pappé writes in *The Idea of Israel* that during the Second Aliyah at the beginning of the twentieth century, "faint-hearted humanist views were not permitted." Walking by an Arab village, Yossef Rabinowitz, a Second Aliyah activist, "found himself ... charmed momentarily by [its] beauty ... and the sound of a shepherd's flute." To snap out of what he described as "a moment of weakness," Rabinowitz reminded himself that "these were foreigners on the homeland." Shavit's great-grandfather and other pioneers "were blessed and cursed," he explains in *My Promised Land*, "with convenient blindness." It was, of course, neither a blessing nor a curse in that God, despite promising them the land, had nothing to do with it. They had been born with sight and hearing and smell, the full range of sensory input, intact, and they developed an ability to suspend what their senses perceived. And if, as he writes, "the historical circumstances were unfavorable," they would tell themselves something else.

For decades after 1948, the Palestinian dispossession foundational to the Zionist project went largely ignored by Israeli historians. During its "war of liberation," Israel was the underdog, its victory nothing short of a miracle. This historiographic erasure mirrored much of what happened on the ground: the destruction of hundreds of villages unfit for a modernizing project, the planting of parks and trees in place of Palestinian homes and cemeteries, the careful renaming, the manufactured disappearance of any sign of Palestinian life. Following the declassification of several documents by the Israeli government in the 1980s, a group of Israeli scholars, calling themselves the "New Historians," reassessed the facts: It turned out that the Palestinians had been the "weaker" side; until the 1940s, the British had armed and supported the Zionists; the Palestinians had not simply "abandoned" their homes; and so on. Historians debated whether the massacres and forced displacement of hundreds of thousands of people were coordinated at the level of Zionist leadership, but they agreed that the state could not have existed had the natives not been dispossessed and significant atrocities not taken place. They collected their thoughts around the question of whether the founding atrocities could be justified—and whether these should reframe everything that followed. Here the New Historians diverged. Historians like Ilan Pappé hoped that if the Israeli public understood the injustice committed against the Palestinians, they might reevaluate the cost of their world. Pappé worked to reform the system from within and, after realizing "most," even if they knew the truth, "would not walk the extra mile that such a position demanded of them," left Israel.

Other Israeli historians, among them Benny Morris, insisted that the Zionist project was a moral necessity. From this, he approached the Nakba with "moral neutrality": unfortunate and unavoidable. Among Morris's most well-known scholarly contributions are *The Birth of the Palestinian Refugee Problem, 1947–1949* (1988) and its revised edition, published in 2004 after Morris uncovered "far more Israeli acts of massacre than [he] had previously thought," and "many cases of rape." Still, in an interview with Ari Shavit published by *Haaretz* in 2004 called "Survival of the Fittest," he asserted:

> [Ben-Gurion] made a serious historical mistake in 1948. Even though he understood the demographic issue and the need to establish a Jewish state without a large Arab minority, he got cold feet during the war . . . If he was already engaged in expulsion, maybe he should have done a complete job.

Shavit, in disbelief, asked Morris to clarify. Did he support the completion of the "transfer" today (in 2004)? Morris offered that he did not, as the present circumstances were not "realistic." There might be a window in the future. "If the threat to Israel is existential, expulsion will be justified." Morris's concerns, then, were tactical. Like Pappé, he understood the "removal" of Palestinians as essential to Zionism. Except Morris chose to stay.

Morris plays out familiar European themes in a conjured Arab mind to dazzling effect. He refers to "the situation" that Zionism faced in 1948 as "genocide," and conflates the "annihilation" of Zionism—a European settler-colonial political project premised on the elimination of the native—with "the annihilation of [his] people." A call to stop, even reverse, the implementation of a genocidal ideology becomes a call to genocide. Political and religious identities merge, reaction precedes action, causality is perfectly inverted, and the danger starts with "the Arabs" *intending* to "destroy the Jews," rather than with Zionist settlers claiming Palestinian land. For Morris, this is why the Palestinians are "not honestly ready" to give up their right of return. They are, he says, "preserving it as an instrument with which they will destroy the Jewish state when the time comes."

Innocence becomes an ontological state. Former Israeli Prime Minister Golda Meir is quoted in her autobiography *A Land of Our Own* as having said, "When peace comes we will perhaps in time be able to forgive the Arabs for killing our sons, but it will be harder for us to forgive them for having forced us to kill their sons." The Israelis are ready for peace, but its arrival is out of their hands, for, she continued, "peace will come when the Arabs will love their children more than they hate us." The Israelis are *forced* to kill children. The Arabs are driven by a totalizing illogic, peace indefinitely deferred. They exist so distanced from their humanity they cannot intuit the biologically hardwired love of their own children. Revolutionary psychiatrist Frantz Fanon writes that settler colonialism is "a systematized negation of the other, a frenzied determination to deny the other any attribute of humanity." Here, as in every colonial encounter, the native's blinding hatred is a stand-in for a causality inconvenient for the occupier. What is most remarkable is that Meir does not attempt to deny the killing of children. Rather she suggests Israel's enemies are responsible for (and bear the consequences of) Israel's actions. And it is this logic legitimizing the obscene, shuffling culpability—all of which I believe she believes—that has been manufactured as state ideology for decades. Today, when Israel commits massacres in Gaza and condemnations ensue, Zionists scream blood libel (and, in *Haaretz*, "Hamas Laid a Genocide Trap for Israel.").

Zionism is a self-contained system of truth, with an origin story inspired by divine right, a bridge over its wretched beginnings. Lord Balfour, author and namesake of the declaration promising Palestine to European Zionists, announced in 1919 that

> the four great powers are committed to Zionism and Zionism, be it right or wrong, good or bad, is rooted in age-long tradition, in present needs, in future hopes, of far profounder import than the desires and prejudices of the 700,000 Arabs who now inhabit that ancient land. In my opinion that is right.

Zionism's solution for the "problem" of the Palestinians is to empty them of any meaning or life that is not self-referential, such that they can be eliminated without triggering remorse, such that the decision to let them stay—on the land, alive, it doesn't matter—becomes an act of benevolence. If the Palestinians are allowed historical grievances (or anything beyond "desires and prejudices"), a consciousness before Zionism, beyond Europe, Zionism collapses. In a sense, Morris is not wrong: Were Palestinians simply allowed to return to their homes, Israel would cease to exist. That they are motivated by what is theirs rather than the wish to destroy Israel, that they fundamentally refuse a world with Europe and its offshoots at its center, is what Morris cannot accept.

Insofar as Palestinians exist, they are *about* Israel. Those uncomfortable with the optics of Zionism measure the condition of its Palestinian subjects as a litmus test for Israel's soul. The titles of their critiques suggest a path to redemption: in the *Jerusalem Post*, "Dehumanizing Palestinians Has Hurt Israel." In *Haaretz*, "If Gaza's Children Starve, Israel Will Lose Its Moral Legitimacy Forever." Or, they warn about the orphaning of Palestinians: *what do you think these poor children will grow up to do, to be?* On the other side of the Zionist coin, the Arabs exist not as fodder for guilt but as the eternal enemy: the human shields and animals, the masses to bomb around election time, on whom to experiment and showcase murderous technology for export. Palestinians exist on the state's periphery, as both mirror and threat, helping Zionists articulate an identity, projected against and shaped by this existential foil (in other words, textbook orientalism). Palestinians are the glue that holds Israel together.

My father, raised during the Israeli siege of Beirut in 1982, shook his head when I asked if Israel's actions in Gaza surprised him. He responded in Arabic, "The Israelis relish in killing us."

The conduct on display in Gaza: part of it is psychological warfare, part of it is colonial theater, part of it is occupation soldiers having fun, and none of it is new. Because the early Zionists failed to do a "complete job," the maintenance of their insecure supremacy over the natives—reinforced through acts of brutality proportional to the degree of human recognition—is a collective struggle. Israeli academic Nurit Peled-Elhanan's *Palestine in Israeli School Books: Ideology and*

*Propaganda in Education* explores how the Israeli education system prepares its children for their compulsory military service, arguing that the cruelty against Palestinians, the "indifference to human suffering, the inflicting of suffering," are its intended consequences. In Israeli grade school text-books, the Arabs—they are called "Palestinian" only in reference to terrorism—appear in general terms, "with a camel . . . vile and deviant and criminal . . . people who don't pay taxes . . . people who don't want to develop." Their mass slaughter during the Nakba is not denied but rather repre-sented as both necessary and good for Israel. Children are taught that Palestinian life is "dispensable with impunity," and that they dispense of Palestinians for Israel's sake: If the Jewish state should survive, these are a people "whose number has to be diminished."

Cradling the Israeli education system is a society that echoes those values. In 2014, settlers in the kibbutzim around Gaza gathered with their families on hilltops—bringing plas-tic chairs and old sofas, popcorn, and hookahs—to watch bombs drop on Palestinian homes. The following year, a group of settlers in the West Bank set a Palestinian home on fire, burning an eighteen-month-old boy and his parents to death; at a wedding sometime after, Israeli settlers recorded themselves dancing with guns, as one repeatedly stabbed a photo of the baby. That same year, a Palestinian child in Jerusalem was kidnapped by settlers, doused with gasoline, and burned alive; two of the three settlers charged with his death were themselves minors. In 2024 at the border with Egypt, settlers blocking aid inflate bounce houses and distribute snacks to soldiers, and a child with an Israeli flag tied around her neck like a cape says to a journalist, "What I care? Kill them. I don't care." These children are conscripted into the Israeli military down the line.

Israel is an anachronism, a settler-colonial work in progress, and that Zionists seem totally unbothered with how we might perceive them reflects a position integral to the project's fabric: tautologically moral, it divides the world into "with us" and "against us," and bulldozes forward with the help of God and foreign politico-economic and military support. It does what it will and presents a potpourri of justifications post-hoc (or, shoot first and ask questions later, in the words of one Israeli official). Zionists have, for over a century, disregarded what it might mean that the Palestinians see them. And their indifference has been maintained by global superpowers—at present, the United States. The Israelis have interpreted this impunity as a *demonstration* of their supremacy, rather than its *basis*, an impunity they wield to showcase strength, even when it appears to us as something closer to fragility.

Zionist supremacy, that perfect bubble, is delicate, requires constant protection in its state of unstable equilibrium. Israel's maneuvering at present—full-blown genocide—reflects a frenzied tripling down of the state's supremacist machinery, to try to restore the bubble atop its shaky hill. What they have over the native is force, and the pleasure it gives, undiminished: the right-wing weekly *Olam Katan* published in January 2024 an article claiming among the great victories of the genocide in Gaza—which it celebrated as unprecedented since the Nakba, even if, it qualified, the Palestinians were exaggerating—is that Israeli culture, previously influenced by "western discourse . . . knows today without shame to rejoice over the deaths of an enemy, and this is said with full mouth. This is decisive moral progress." Israel is a small place and because the majority of Israelis want the native gone, they cannot look away, and because theirs is a society structured around its military, they do not have to: They learn to see the Palestinian through the scope of a gun.

Looking at Israelis looking at Palestinians, it is easier to imagine they cannot see than to consider what it means for them to know. We psychologize, in some ways, to avoid having to. Settler psychosis, sick society, *these people are not in their right minds*—these are descriptive terms that reflect our inability to make sense, within a particular ethical or moral frame, of what *we* see; they do not interrogate etiology. The *illness*, given its prevalence, must be colonization: Through contagion or side effect, the brutality of colonialism folds back on the colonizer. The occupation exacts a price on its enforcers. Missing is historical time, through which we see that the problem starts with the decision to colonize. A tweet, by a doctor, advises us to avoid "dehumanizing" Israelis. She suggests we instead consider their behavior to reflect a complex trauma response to entrapment in cyclical violence. But alienation is only possible because we already perceive the actor as a human being. The language of illness confuses morality with mental status and diffuses blame. It erases volition, without which there is neither escape nor responsibility.

Understanding Zionism as a product and function of people does not quite show us the door. That is why, I think, the world met the actions of Aaron Bushnell, the active-duty US Airforce member who lit himself on fire outside the Israeli embassy in Washington, DC, with something like a burst of recognition: Under the snarled weight of seemingly inescapable structural pull, here was a person stepping forward, disentangling their agency at the greatest cost to try to map the gravity of refusing to do so. The last time an Israeli self-immolated for geopolitical reasons was in 2005, in protest of the "evacuation" order from Gaza.

One cannot erase what they do not see. Ari Shavit's great-grandfather knew, Lord Balfour knew, Ben-Gurion knew, the people in the kibbutzim knew, and every soldier in Gaza knows. And the people back home, they know too. In the years since 1917 or 1948 or 1982, Zionism has become increasingly difficult to maintain, and requires a certain insularity—sustained by the United States—that appears, if rooted in a less curated selection of facts and causal links, like insanity. For Israelis, this is self-preservation. Peering into the Zionist project, what we see is what Zionism requires.

# 5

## On the Parallel Annexation
## of the West Bank

*Mariam Barghouti*

I was not surprised it happened. Anyone familiar with the region, and with the reality endured by Palestinians, could see it was only a matter of time. Given the geopolitical dynamics, it was never a question of *if*, but *when* Palestinians would erupt in confrontation against the Israeli colonial regime. What shocked Palestinians, Israelis, and the world wasn't the response itself, but the fact that a small group of militants—raised in what amounts to an open-air prison—briefly ruptured Israel's security apparatus. The Palestinian-led offensive was the first of its kind, in scale and impact, since the creation of the State of Israel in 1948. It marked the most significant and unique event in contemporary Palestinian history. At least 1,200 Israelis were killed. According to a list published by the *Times of Israel*, at least 497 of those killed were active members of Israel's military, police, and intelligence forces.

Palestinians in Gaza may have anticipated such an event. In the days leading up to it, protests near the apartheid wall surrounding the Gaza Strip had been escalating. But because of Israel's strategic fragmentation of Palestinian communities, Palestinians in the West Bank, Jerusalem, and historic Palestine had no idea what was unfolding. How could they? Gaza is sealed off by a labyrinth of identity cards, concrete barriers, checkpoints, military bases, and settlements. Meanwhile, those outside the open-air prison were busy confronting an increasingly violent expansionist regime.

As the media scrambled to cover the offensive—focusing on Israeli fatalities and framing the attack as a terrorist assault involving babies allegedly burned alive or beheaded—Palestinians held their breath.

Those forty-eight hours after October 7 were charged. Everyone, especially Palestinians, was shaken. Had Palestinians really just killed hundreds of Israelis at once? Had the Palestinians imprisoned in Gaza really managed to break the seemingly unbreakable prison walls? For weeks, roads in the West Bank, East Jerusalem, and Palestinian towns inside Israel were deserted. People stayed indoors, gripped by fear of Israeli retaliation. Everyone knew what was coming. Everyone knew *it was coming.*

The fear was clear: extermination.

This fear wasn't born in a vacuum. Even before October 7, Israel's settler-military system was intensifying attacks on Palestinians in the West Bank and Jerusalem. Just six months earlier, Israel's national security minister, Itamar Ben-Gvir, had called for "Operation Defensive Shield 2," referencing the early 2000s military campaign during which Israeli forces launched large-scale assaults on Palestinian towns in a bid to crush resistance and accelerate annexation.

Language cannot adequately convey the brutality of a regime emboldened by slogans like "Death to Arabs" and "the second Nakba is coming." To capture the scale of abuse, I focus here on events I witnessed in the West Bank, where I live, over the past three years—the days that laid the groundwork for Israel's ongoing campaign of ravaging Gaza and beyond.

In March 2020, the World Health Organization formally declared COVID-19 a global pandemic. By 2024, the virus had claimed at least 7 million lives worldwide. Yet, even amid a global health emergency, Palestinians remained subject to Israeli repression.

Just four months into the pandemic, Prime Minister Benjamin Netanyahu announced a new phase of annexation, promising to legalize the illegal Israeli outposts that had sprung up across the West Bank and to annex the Jordan Valley, which makes up nearly a third of the West Bank.

In Gaza, Palestinians faced the pandemic in what is effectively a cage. Denied access to proper medical care and packed into one of the most densely populated areas on Earth, they faced heightened risk of infection. Palestinian detainees, meanwhile, were deprived of water, hygiene products, and nutrition. In interviews with released prisoners, I learned they were given half an orange for vitamin C, sometimes denied meals altogether, and provided with no masks.

Elsewhere, Syrian Druze in the occupied Golan Heights began protesting Israel's "Genesis Wind Project." Developed by Enlight Renewable Energy, the project is Israel's largest renewable energy initiative, comprising thirty-nine General Electric wind turbines. Druze residents voiced concerns over its environmental, health, and territorial impacts.

At the same time, Palestinians in Sheikh Jarrah, a neighborhood in East Jerusalem, faced intensifying violence aimed at forcing them from their homes. The families in the occupied Golan and Sheikh Jarrah appealed for support.

Protests spread quickly. What began as localized resistance to wind turbines evolved into a wave of nonviolent resistance against Israel's systemic violations of Palestinian and Syrian rights. By early May 2021, Israel's violent response to the protests escalated. In mid-May, Hamas launched a campaign called "The Sword of Jerusalem," as a response to Israel's intensification of abuse, particularly in Jerusalem. Rather than cease its violations, Israel expanded the scope of its abuse with "Operation Guardian of the Walls," an eleven-day offensive that killed at least 261 Palestinians in Gaza, 67 of whom were children.

Yet, mass protests erupted in Ramallah, Nablus, Hebron, Haifa, Jaffa, the Golan Heights, and Gaza. The message was clear: end the settler-colonial expansion. In a manifesto that came to be known as the Intifada of Hope and Unity, Palestinians declared:

*People of Palestine,*
    *Here we are, writing a new chapter of courage and pride, in which we tell a story of justice and of the truth that no level of*

*Israeli colonial repression can erase, however cruel and brutal that repression may be . . .*

*This is how Israel imprisoned us in prisons of isolation; some of us caged in the "Oslo prison" in the West Bank, some in the "citizenship prison" in the part of Palestine occupied in 1948, some of us isolated by the monstrous siege and ongoing, devastating assault on the "Gaza prison," some of us isolated under the systematic Judaization campaigns on the "Jerusalem prison," and some isolated from Palestine altogether, dispersed across all corners of the globe.*

In response to Israel's assault on Gaza, and as part of the Intifada of Hope and Unity, Palestinians called for a general strike—the largest since 1936—uniting people in the West Bank, Gaza, and those holding Israeli citizenship. Young people were quickly targeted. In the West Bank, the Palestinian Authority (PA) collaborated with Israel in a campaign of intimidation: unlawful arrests, torture, and threats against families.

Meanwhile, within Israel, Prime Minister Netanyahu authorized the use of lethal force against anyone "causing chaos," launching what he dubbed "Operation Law and Order." Already subjected to systemic discrimination, they bore the brunt of Operation Law and Order. That summer made one thing unmistakably clear: no document could protect Palestinians from the power of the Israeli state.

In June 2021, PA critic and Palestinian Legislative Council candidate Nizar Banat revealed a secret agreement between the PA and Israeli government to distribute expired COVID-19 vaccines to Palestinians. Weeks later, Banat was beaten to death in his home by PA security forces, in front of his wife and children. Though officials claimed an investigation took place, within a year, all suspects had been released.

The pandemic revealed a grim truth: Palestinians were on their own. Not even global catastrophe could shield them from violence—not from Israel, and not from their own leadership.

And yet, in September 2021, Palestinians woke to astonishing news. On September 6, six detainees escaped from Gilboa Prison, one of Israel's most secure facilities. Using makeshift tools, they dug a tunnel and emerged outside. The prisoners—from Jenin, Ara, and Nablus[1]—were soon recaptured and subjected to intensified torture, solitary confinement, and denied access to lawyers or family. But they left a message behind: "We are living in graves."

In 2022, Palestinian resistance in the West Bank escalated.

Youth in refugee camps across the northern West Bank, many of whom had been formerly detained and tortured by Israel, began engaging in armed confrontations against increasing settler violence. Once again, Israel responded with violence. I remember the image clearly: a car torn apart by bullets in Nablus, the street soaked in blood and scorched car metal. The men inside were executed without trial or due

---

1    Although the men are residents of the West Bank, they are refugees, some of whom—like Zachariah Zubeidi—grew up in the Jenin refugee camp, but are originally from towns and villages which were depopulated by Zionist militias between 1947–49.

process. Yet, their killing marked the emergence of a new and organized armed group: the Lions' Den.

Just a month later, in direct response to growing Palestinian mobilization since 2021, the Israeli military launched "Operation Break the Wave." A joint effort with Israeli police and intelligence units, it also included the Palestinian Authority and was aimed at suppressing Palestinian resistance. Meanwhile, settlers accelerated their efforts to annex Palestinian land. Displacement rates doubled between 2022 and 2023. In fact, from 2020 to 2024, the number of Palestinians displaced by Israel surged by 324 percent.

Arrests rose sharply. Palestinians were detained on charges ranging from posting on social media to stone throwing— even for belonging to a political party, a right protected under international law. More alarmingly, there was a spike in administrative detention: imprisonment without charge or trial, denying Palestinians even the opportunity to defend themselves. How does one contest an accusation that's never shared?

Meanwhile, Israeli settlements and outposts continued to expand—across Area C and into Areas A and B. Violent settler incursions surged in the northern West Bank: Jenin, Tulkarem, Nablus, Salfit. Despite the PA's jurisdiction over Area A, its leadership did nothing to either stop the land grabs or protect civilians from paramilitary settler mobs. On the contrary, the acting PA president authorized the use of weapons by Palestinian security forces—against Palestinians resisting Israeli military operations. This was especially evident in Nablus and Jenin, which had become hubs of organized armed resistance.

On the morning of August 9, 2022, the city of Nablus woke to the sound of explosions and drones. Ibrahim al-Nabulsi—dubbed "the lion of Nablus"—was killed in a large-scale Israeli military operation under the pretext of eliminating a "senior terrorist." He had been close friends with the three men executed earlier that year. Al-Nabulsi's death followed a settler-led media campaign calling for his assassination. His "crime" was engaging in armed resistance against settlers who had stormed Joseph's Tomb—located in an area officially under full Palestinian control. Al-Nabulsi was eighteen years old.

His murder, along with that of Islam Subuh (thirty-two years old) and Hussein Taha (sixteeen), marked a turning point. In the months that followed, the West Bank witnessed a surge in armed resistance—especially in the north. These groups were largely composed of third-generation refugees: young men who had grown up under occupation, repeatedly detained and tortured by Israeli soldiers, denied education and jobs, forced to labor for settlers or endure poverty. They had, expectedly, reached a breaking point.

During the pandemic, when Israel further tightened the issuance of work permits for Palestinians, it became clear how the most basic aspects of daily life, and survival, is utterly dependent on Israeli policies. The men began reclaiming agency. In Jenin refugee camp, resistance groups emerged that transcended political affiliations. Their only allegiance was to resistance and the pursuit of freedom.

I met many of them. Interviewed their families. Watched, helpless, as they were executed one by one in extrajudicial killings. Israel labeled them terrorists but overlooked a crucial fact: it was Israeli forces conducting raids on their towns, launching drone strikes and air raids, reducing neighborhoods to rubble, and killing children and unarmed civilians alongside their intended targets. It was Israel that was fragmenting and unbinding every aspect of these men's lives. These men were being hunted—for resisting imprisonment in their own homes, for daring to choose a life with dignity. Most of the men I interviewed shared the same dream: "I want to go to the beach without a soldier stopping me. I want to raise my children without the risk of a settler coming to rip them apart."

As Israel intensified its campaigns in Gaza, it began deploying the same tactics in the West Bank. During my field reporting, I heard accounts of unfamiliar weapons being used in flashpoint areas like Nablus and Tulkarem. In October 2022—soon dubbed "the bloodiest month," with thirty Palestinians killed—a young man told me of a drone "that looked like the surveillance ones we know, but this one was shooting bullets at us." I tried to verify his story but found no public record. Later, it emerged that Israel had begun using a new weapon: the "quadcopter," part of Elbit Systems' Legion-X platform, publicly revealed only in November 2022.

By 2023, life for Palestinians was defined by systemic violence, daily loss, and policies engineered to grind down any will to resist.

I was alarmed by the scale of violence. In just the first three months of 2023, Israel increased Palestinian displacement by 78 percent. I couldn't keep up with the demolitions. Everywhere I went, people described their lives in the same terms: "It feels like a new Nakba." Settlers marched through Palestinian towns chanting: "A second Nakba is coming."

For Palestinians, Nakba means not just expulsion—but mass death.

Even before the genocide, the first half of 2023 became the deadliest period for Palestinians since the UN began recording fatalities in 2005. Nearly half of all those killed in the West Bank that year died within those three months. Among them were unprecedented numbers of children.

I reviewed autopsy reports: the overwhelming majority showed kill shots to the head and chest. In some cases, the bodies were so riddled with bullets that the cause of death was unclear. Perhaps it was the bullet that hit their artery, perhaps it was the one in their head, perhaps it was all of them at once. Videos of teenage boys shot dead in the street became common. The sound of mothers wailing became daily background noise.

Palestinians were shot at checkpoints, while driving, while playing, while praying. They were arrested in the night, police dogs unleashed on them. Children in refugee camps were systemically wounded by bullets fired from military towers strategically built at the edge of nearly every town and village in the West Bank.

At the same time, Israel waged a political campaign to erase Palestinian claims to the land. Refugee camps were labelled terror hubs. With US support, they were turned into zones of military experimentation—surveilled, raided, starved, destroyed, and eventually emptied.

Families began sleeping in houses outside the camps to escape nightly raids. By day, they returned to find homes demolished or abandoned. With no camps left, Israel could claim there were no refugees. Just as it has insisted since 1948 that Palestinians "fled," it would now say the same of those in the West Bank—discrediting not only their right to return but erasing the traces of their existence.

By mid-2023, Palestinians braced for a full-scale invasion of the West Bank and Jerusalem. Before Ben-Gvir's "Operation Defensive Shield 2" could materialize, the world's attention turned southwest. On October 7, men on paragliders descended on settlements near Gaza.

In the West Bank, we watched in paralysis. We knew what would come—because it had already come for us. The quad-copters used in Gaza had first been tested in Nablus. The home raids and hospital bombings—those, too, we had seen in Jenin, Ramallah, and Tulkarem. The children riddled with bullets became children bombed to dust.

And still, Israel didn't stop. It never stops. It advances with impunity, obliterating people, trees, animals—everything in its path.

Israel does not value Palestinian life. It would rather see us in body bags than acknowledge our right to live freely on our land. In Gaza, where 70 percent of the population are refugees, the violence is even more ferocious. For Palestinians, Israel's message is clear: be displaced, or die.

# 6

## "A war against everyone in Gaza": Transcripts from *The Night Won't End* and *Starving Gaza*

### Laila Al-Arian

"This war destroyed everything. Houses, people, trees, stones," said Hanan Assaf, a mother in Gaza. "Everything was destroyed."

Hanan's two-year-old son, Khaled, can be seen in a video on her cell phone, running around kicking a bouncy green ball, his cheeks round and chubby. But in photos taken months later, his cheeks look sunken, his tiny body withering away from a lack of food. As Israel tightened its already crippling siege of Gaza after October 7, all the Assaf family had to eat at times was *khubaiza*, a wild green. "The boy looked like a skeleton. He was gone. He was completely gone. I would hold him like a newborn. He stopped being able to sit up, move or walk. His body became very weak," Hanan recalled sitting in her son's room, surrounded by rubble and ash. "The occupation forces burned it. They didn't leave us a single memory. Nothing." In February 2024, just a few months into Israel's assault on Gaza, Hanan and her husband,

Muhammad, buried Khaled. "Before the war, we thought about how our children would get married and go to college. We thought about the future," Hanan told my team at Al Jazeera English. "Now, we only think about how to get food and water for our children. That's it."

It didn't take long after Israel launched its brutal onslaught on Gaza to see that this was a war on life itself. The occupation forces destroyed everything that gives and sustains life: universities, schools, mosques, churches, bakeries, hospitals and homes, so many homes. They attacked water stations, fishing boats, aid convoys, children getting water, adults lining up for flour, people burying their dead, grandmothers waving white flags. They sniped children in the head and heart and executed men point-blank in front of their wives and children. They didn't even leave the dead in peace, as they bulldozed over graveyards and dug up bodies—repeatedly.

"This war destroyed everything" has become a haunting refrain on the tongues of the Palestinians of Gaza, whether they are on the ground or in the diaspora, surrounded by destroyed buildings turned into rubble or watching footage of their beloved city become a shell of what it once was: the places where they got married, gave birth, bought clothing for special occasions, ate memorable meals, and celebrated graduations, all gone.

After October 7, while it attacked Gaza from the air, ground, and sea, Israel turned the city into a killing cage, where every Palestinian, no matter their age or status in life, was considered an enemy, a legitimate target for slaughter.

Everyone in Gaza knows that nowhere in Gaza is safe. Not homes, or hospitals, or schools repurposed as shelters or tent cities for the endlessly displaced. And yet, it is a human instinct to try to save your life—and your children's.

Wissam Hamada was from Al-Wehda Street, a major thoroughfare in central Gaza City. After October 7, she was displaced to ten different homes, along with her husband and two children, six-year-old Hind Rajab and her brother Eyad, who was four. The first time they fled it was because leaflets that fell from the sky ordered them to leave. Each time they would shelter in a place, they found that safety was elusive. They were besieged by Israeli forces or faced violent airstrikes. The night was particularly frightening because it was when the pounding was especially loud. "When night falls, it feels endless. You wake up all night wondering, 'Will the morning arrive?' It's even worse for children," Wissam said.

One day, as they were sheltering in south Gaza on orders from the Israeli military, Wissam's mother asked her to write her name and ID number on her hands so that she could be identified in case she were killed. That was enough for Wissam to decide that she would rather die in Gaza City, where people already knew her, than as a stranger in an unfamiliar place. "My husband told me to stay. I told him I'm afraid. I want to go back to my home and if I'm killed I want it to be known it was me, that I'm Wissam Hamada," she said.

Wissam's husband decided to stay behind in the south with her parents. "I didn't think we'd be separated for

long. I thought the war would end in two to three days,"
she said.

Before October 7, Wissam lived a simple life with her
husband, parents-in-law, and children. Her daughter, Hind,
was the light of her life, with her wavy brown hair and sweet
smile. She loved school and hoped one day to become a
dentist.

When she arrived back to Gaza City, Wissam found herself
surrounded by the Israeli military. She sheltered with around
100 relatives, more than half of whom were children. "There
isn't a place that they invaded that wasn't close to us," she
said. "We were besieged for entire days. We spent six days at
home. We couldn't move freely at home when they invaded
Al-Wehda Street. We couldn't move at all. They attacked any
movement." She said Israeli soldiers were stationed right
outside of their door for a full day, firing into the house as the
terrified children's screams grew louder. "Why would you
open fire on the home? Did we go out armed? Did we do
anything for you to attack us like this? All you heard was a
child's voice," she said. It didn't matter that at the time, the
military had told them that Al-Wehda Street was a "safe
zone." Wissam had seen this before repeatedly, safe zones
attacked, cars shot at, buildings reduced to rubble, and body
parts strewn on streets the Israelis had promised them were
safe passages.

On the night of January 28, 2024, Wissam and her children
were trying to sleep when they heard heavy attacks by Israeli
forces. The fire belt bombings were so intense, Wissam said.
The blaze reached their home, forcing them to move to the

middle of the house. Afraid of what would happen, she asked Hind, whom she had nicknamed Hannoud, to sleep next to her. Wissam had a feeling of dread. "While her eyes were closed, I was looking at her, thinking, 'God, how beautiful you are. Are you really going to leave me, Hannoud? No, stay here.'" Wissam recalled, "I never loved anyone as much as I loved my daughter Hind."

The next morning, Wissam and some of her relatives decided to leave in search of safety, while it was still calm. It was cold and raining heavily. Wissam's uncle, his wife, and fifteen-year-old daughter, Layan, took their car to flee. Hind rode with them to avoid the bad weather. Eyad almost did, too, but jumped out at the last minute to stay with his mother.

Soon after they left, the car was fired on by Israeli forces. Wissam could hear witnesses scream for an ambulance. She said bystanders tried to reach the car but it was too dangerous. There were too many soldiers and tanks. She called her uncle's cell phone again and again and Layan finally answered. She told her that her parents had been killed and that she and Hind were still alive but injured and bleeding. Their relatives reached the Palestine Red Crescent Society in Ramallah to ask them to dispatch a team in Gaza to rescue the girls. When a dispatcher named Omar reached Layan, she told him that an Israeli tank was continuing to fire at the car. In a phone recording of their conversation, Layan could be heard screaming in terror and then the line goes silent.

Omar called back and this time Hind picked up. She told him that Layan had been killed, and he told her to hide under the seats in the car. Hind confirmed to him that the Israeli tank was still next to the car and asked the rescue workers to help her. The Red Crescent spent hours trying to coordinate access to the site with Israeli authorities, as Hind remained on the line, on and off, begging them to come. When Wissam was able to connect to Hind, she tried to comfort her terrified daughter, telling her she loved her, and that help would be coming soon. She and the Red Crescent workers also read verses of the Quran to comfort and distract Hind, as she recited along.

After three hours, the Israelis agreed to allow rescue workers in Gaza to go to the area, which was near a gas station in Gaza City, and even sent them a map with an approved route. The sun was down by the time the two paramedics, Ahmed Al-Madhoun and Yousef Zeino, headed to the scene. As they spoke to their colleagues in Ramallah, a loud sound could be heard in the background and then the line cut out. Hind, still on the line, confirmed that she heard a boom. "Her 'yes' means our colleagues who went to rescue her had died," said Nisreen Qawas, the Red Crescent's director of mental health.

Hind's voice grew fainter, and her mother began to grow more worried. She told Wissam that she wasn't speaking because her mouth was bleeding. When her mother told Hind to wipe the blood with her hand, Hind's response was "I don't want to get my shirt dirty, so I don't trouble my mom." Wissam told her, "It's ok, wipe your mouth and I'll wash it, my sweetheart." She agreed but then her voice disappeared completely. It was 7:00 p.m.

Still, Wissam maintained hope, going to Al-Ahli Baptist Hospital and praying that each arriving ambulance would bring Hind. Civil defense workers later found the car Hind and her family were in ridden with more than 300 bullet holes. The ambulance was an eviscerated and burned-out shell. Only one of the paramedics' skulls was found, along with other bones.

Wissam tried to stay strong for her remaining child, Eyad. "It's impossible that anyone was as devastated as I was when I heard her voice, saying, 'Come get me,'" Wissam said through tears, "I couldn't get to my daughter. It's the most difficult feeling in the world to hear my daughter ask me to go get her when I can't reach her. My sweetheart, I swear I couldn't reach you. Forgive me. Forgive me, sweetheart. I couldn't reach Hind."

Her mind races with thoughts about Hind's final moments. *What was the last thing she saw? Did she see tanks? Did she see soldiers? Did she see bullets? Warplanes? Whatever she saw would be unbearable for an adult, let alone a child.* "So how did my daughter, at her age, manage to handle seeing it?"

Hind Rajab's case, a six-year-old child pleading for her life, shocked the world. But it didn't lead to any justice or accountability for those who killed her. According to researchers at Forensic Architecture, the Merkava tank that fired at Hind and her family likely had optical equipment that would have allowed the soldiers to see who they were shooting at. What possible rules of engagement can justify shooting at a car full of civilians, including fifteen- and six-year-old girls? In what universe is firing at paramedics, let alone ones who had been cleared by Israeli authorities to rescue Hind, a legitimate claim of self-defense? As disturbing as the details of Hind's story are, it is unremarkable in Gaza, where women, children, and the elderly make up the majority of the casualties and hundreds of healthcare workers have been killed.

Throughout the genocide in Gaza, there have been viral moments and famous cases like Hind's that, for a moment, so horrified people that it seemed like maybe a shift in global opinion would put enough pressure on Israel to stop. There was the burning alive of Shaban al-Dalou, the nineteen-year-old who was photographed engulfed in flames while still hooked up to an IV, his arms flailing desperately in the air. There was also Abdullah Al-Ghaf, the father who went to the market to get his hungry two-year-old some biscuits only to return to find the toddler and his mother had been killed in a strike. A video showed a sobbing Abdullah putting the biscuits by his tiny son's shroud. There are also the haunting images of child after child whose limbs were cut off in violent attacks in what is now considered the largest number per capita of child amputees in modern history. There are too many videos to count of parents sobbing over their dead children and children crying for the parents they lost. And how does one see video after video without concluding that this cruelty is the point, that there is no bottom to Israel's campaign of extermination?

As Nisreen, from the Red Crescent said, "What makes it more difficult for me, is that, is it only Hind? Are there another 1,000 Hind stories? 10,000 Hind stories that did not have a name and a story on the TV?" Hind Rajab became a symbol for the dehumanization and brutality of the Israeli state toward Palestinians, conducting what is likely to be the most documented mass killing campaign in history, a live-streamed genocide that is simultaneously normalized by the world's powers and impossible to look away from for those with a conscience.

The genocide of Gaza is one of the latest manifestations of the ongoing Nakba of 1948, the killing and forced displacement of Palestinians that came with the creation of Israel on stolen land. The impact of the Nakba reverberated deeply with the generation that survived it and their descendants. What then will become of the Palestinians who were injured, maimed, orphaned, displaced, and terrorized in this genocide?

In November 2024, Hossam Shabat, a journalist from north Gaza, wrote online about a friend of his father's whom he ran into on the street but did not recognize immediately. "No one looks the same after a year of genocide," he posted. "I asked him how he had been doing. He said he had four sons, and one after another, they were killed over the span of a year. His last son and wife were killed last month. Now, he sleeps on the streets with no family. A vibrant man who once owned a house, a car, and a business is now deprived of everything, even his family." Israel has wiped out hundreds of families in Gaza from the civil registry, and it is not unusual to hear about parents losing most of their children or the new term that was born during this war on Gaza: "Wounded child, no surviving family."

The evidence establishing that Israel's war is against all the people of Gaza has come not just from the victims, but the perpetrators as well, with video after video showing Israeli soldiers blowing up empty mosques, burning humanitarian aid meant for starved people, and vandalizing shops and homes, for no justifiable reason other than to satisfy their sadistic impulses. There has been enough testimony from Israeli soldiers to demonstrate that they have entered Gaza with the firm belief that their enemy is the Palestinian people themselves, and that mission is to make Gaza uninhabitable, to kill, destroy, displace, annihilate.

It is not enough to bear witness to these crimes when the truth of them is obscured with tired, racist canards and justifications that are verifiably untrue: that Hamas hides behind civilians, that none of these killings happened because Palestinians make them up, that every Palestinian death is the fault of their own people. The least we can do for the victims of this violence is to call it what it really is: the intentional destruction of a group of people, in whole or in part. A genocide.

Hind Rajab's brother, Eyad, may be four, but his mother says, "The pain he is carrying is that of someone more than twenty." He walks around with a doll that he named after his sister. Wissam said that the little boy cannot accept Hind's absence. She has no hope that a world order that claims to care about human rights will ever do anything for her family. "I never felt that international laws or international organizations ever did anything for Gaza. It's just ink on paper," she said. "They didn't protect paramedics, journalists, children, or civilians. Hind, Layan, my uncle, his wife and children were executed in cold blood."

# How to Spot a Genocide

## Mona Chalabi

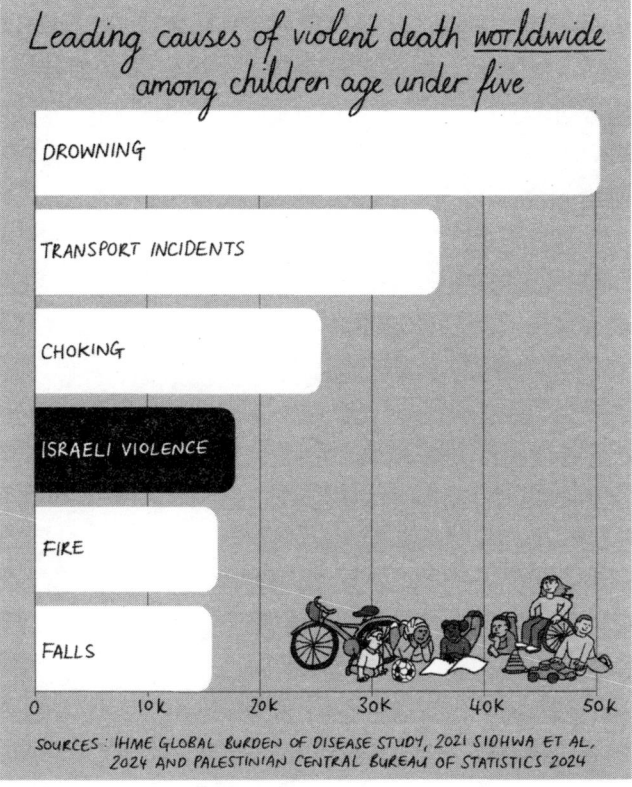

Leading causes of violent death worldwide among children age under five

- DROWNING
- TRANSPORT INCIDENTS
- CHOKING
- ISRAELI VIOLENCE
- FIRE
- FALLS

0    10k    20k    30k    40k    50k

SOURCES: IHME GLOBAL BURDEN OF DISEASE STUDY, 2021 SIDHWA ET AL. 2024 AND PALESTINIAN CENTRAL BUREAU OF STATISTICS 2024

# 7
## Unsafe Passage
### *Mosab Abu Toha*

When the war comes to Gaza, my wife and I do not want to leave. We want to be with our parents and brothers and sisters, and we know that to leave Gaza is to leave them. Even when the border with Egypt opens to people with foreign passports, like our three-year-old son, Mostafa, we stay. Our apartment in Beit Lahia, in northern Gaza, is on the third floor. My brothers live above and below us, and my parents live on the ground floor. My father cares for chickens and rabbits in the garden. I have a library filled with books that I love.

Then Israel drops flyers on our neighborhood, warning us to evacuate, and we crowd into a borrowed two-bedroom apartment in the Jabalia refugee camp. Soon, we learn that a bomb has destroyed our house. Air strikes also rain down on the camp, killing dozens of people within a hundred meters of our door. Over time, our parents stop telling us to stay.

When our apartment in the refugee camp is no longer a refuge, we move again, to a United Nations Relief and Works

Agency (UNRWA) school. My wife, Maram, sleeps in a classroom with dozens of women and children. I sleep outside, with the men, exposed to the dew. Once, I hear a piece of shrapnel ring through the school, as though a teacup has fallen off a table.

Now, when Maram and I talk about leaving, we understand that the decision is not only about us. It is about our three children. In Gaza, a child is not really a child. Our eight-year-old son, Yazzan, has been talking about fetching his toys from the ruins of our house. He should be learning how to draw, how to play soccer, how to take a family photo. Instead, he is learning how to hide when bombs fall.

On November 4, our names appear on an approved list of travelers at the Rafah border crossing, clearing us to leave Gaza. The next day, we set out on foot, joining a wave of Palestinians making the thirty-kilometer journey south. Those who can travel faster than us, on donkeys and tuktuks, soon come into view again, traveling toward us. We see a friend, who tells us that Israeli forces have set up a checkpoint on Salah al-Din Road, the north-south highway that is supposed to provide safe passage. He says that gunfire there convinced him to turn around. We return to the school.

Mostafa and Yaffa, our six-year-old daughter, are so sick with fever that they can barely walk. My sisters have also been asking us not to go. "Let's not leave them," Maram says. We want to stay for our family, and we want to leave for our family.

Then, on November 15, I am on the third floor of the school, about to sip some tea, when I hear a blast followed by screams. A type of shell that we call a smoke bomb has gone off outside. People are trying to put out a fire by dousing it with sand.

Moments later, another smoke bomb explodes in the sky above us, spewing a white cloud of gas. We race inside, coughing, and shut the doors and windows. Maram hands out pieces of wet cloth and we hold them to our noses and mouths, trying to breathe.

That night, we hear bombs and tank shells, and I barely sleep. In the days that follow, my throat tastes of gas and I have diarrhea. I cannot find a clean toilet. There is no water to flush. I feel like vomiting.

I have been joking with my family that by my thirty-first birthday, on November 17, we will have peace. When the day arrives, I am embarrassed. I ask my mother, "Where is my cake?" She says she will bake one when she moves back into our destroyed house.

On November 18, Israeli tank shells wreck two classrooms at another school, where Maram's grandparents and paternal uncles are staying. My brother-in-law Ahmad learns that several members of his extended family are dead. My parents urge us not to leave our shelter. But, when we hear the news, we pretend to go to the bathroom and go looking for our relatives.

On the dusty road that leads to the school, a heartbreaking scene greets us. People are fleeing with gas cannisters, mattresses, and blankets. A group of donkeys and horses are bleeding. One horse's tail is nearly detached. When a young man tries to quench its thirst, the water dribbles out of a hole in its neck. He asks me whether I have a knife, to put it out of its misery.

We are relieved to find Maram's grandparents inside, sitting on the floor. As her uncles pack their things, one of them talks about fleeing to the south. Maram's grandparents are pleading with him not to go.

The next morning, I wake at five to an overcast sky. A storm is coming. While everyone is sleeping, I fill a bottle of water from an open bucket, wash, and pray the dawn prayer. Then, at around 6:30 a.m., Maram's uncle Nader comes to our room. He is preparing to leave for the south with his brothers. "If anyone wants to join, we will be at the gate of the hospital," he says.

This time, when I ask Maram whether she wants to go, she says yes. "All our bags are packed," she tells me.

Maram informs her parents of our decision. They cry as she hugs them. Then we both go to the third floor, where my parents are sitting in the corridor on a mattress. They are drinking their morning coffee with two of my sisters and their husbands. I squat, and in a low voice I tell my parents that we are going to try to leave Gaza.

My mother goes pale. She looks at my children, tears in her eyes.

I don't want to hug anyone, because I don't want to believe that I am leaving them. I kiss my parents and shake hands with my siblings, as though I am only going on a short trip. What I am feeling is not guilt but a sense of unfairness. Why can I leave and they cannot? We are lucky that Mostafa was born in the United States. Does it make them less human, less worthy of protection, that their children were not? I think about how, when we go, I may not be able to call them or even find out whether they are alive or dead. Every step we take will take us away from them.

Before Maram was my wife, she was my neighbor. In 2000, when I was eight, my father moved us out of my birthplace, Al-Shati refugee camp, and built us the house in Beit Lahia. Maram, a year younger than me, lived next door. I liked her enough that, each school year, I gave her my old textbooks so she wouldn't have to buy new ones.

One day, Maram saw me on the third floor of our family home, peering into the distance through a new pair of binoculars. From our window, I could see the border with Israel. She sent her younger sister to ask me whether I was looking for a girl.

I told Maram's sister that it was none of her business. After that, though, I knew Maram had feelings for me. We started to smuggle one another messages via our little sisters. In 2015, when I was twenty-two, we married.

On the morning that we set out for the south, Maram wears a jilbab and carries Yaffa's blanket, which has the head of a fox and two sleeves, so she can wear it like a cape. We have one liter of water. By the time we gather our things and walk to the hospital gate with Maram's youngest brother, Ibrahim, her uncles have already left.

I hail a teenager who is driving a donkey cart. "Going south?"

He has no idea which way is south. "How much will you pay me?" he asks.

I offer a hundred Israeli shekels, about twenty-seven US dollars. Another young man, whose mother uses a wheelchair, splits the cost with us.

Our donkey cart rolls past bombed-out houses and shops. The street is a river of people flowing south, many of them carrying white flags to identify themselves as civilians. Ibrahim jumps off the donkey cart, picks up a stick, and ties a white undershirt to it.

In the crowd, I see a man named Rami, who played soccer with me more than a decade ago. He cries out with joy and asks whether his seventy-year-old father can climb into our cart. We make some space and ride on.

About thirteen kilometers into our journey, we pass Al-Kuwait Square. An Israeli checkpoint looms in the distance. Soldiers are controlling the flow of foot traffic with a tank and a sand barrier. When the soldiers want to block the way, they roll the tank onto the road.

Hundreds of people, young and old, crowd the road in front of the tank. I can think of one other scene like this—the Nakba of 1948, when Zionist militias forced hundreds of thousands of Palestinians to leave their villages and towns. In photographs from that time, families flee on foot, balancing what remains of their belongings on their heads.

The children are scared. Mostafa asks me if he can go back north again to his grandmother Iman, who used to tuck him into bed. I don't know what to tell him. We are going to see her, I finally say. Be patient.

As we near the tank, I hold up our stack of travel documents, with Mostafa's blue American passport on top. One of the soldiers in the tank is shouting into a megaphone; another holds a machine gun. I have lived in Gaza for almost all my life, and these are the first Israeli soldiers I have seen. I am not afraid of them, but I will be soon.

We are overjoyed to spot, up ahead of us, Maram's uncles. Ibrahim shouts out. One of them, Amjad, grins and yells back, "You made it!"

The line crawls along. One of Maram's great-uncles, Fayez, is pushing a wheelchair carrying Maram's ninety-year-old great-grandmother. To my surprise, Fayez convinces the soldiers that elders should go through first, with one person to accompany them. But, when two people try to accompany one wheelchair, a soldier angrily orders them to stop. He fires his gun into the ground.

Children scream. Panic ripples through the line. A gust of wind blows, as if to rearrange the stage of the theater. The tank rolls back onto the road, and about twenty minutes elapse before it backs up again.

We are about to pass the checkpoint when a soldier starts to call out, seemingly at random.

"The young man with the blue plastic bag and the yellow jacket, put everything down and come here."

"The man with white hair and a boy in his arms, leave everything and come!"

They're not going to pull me out of the line, I think. I am holding Mostafa and flashing his American passport. Then the soldier says, "The young man with the black backpack who is carrying a red-haired boy. Put the boy down and come my way." He is talking to me.

I make the sudden decision to try to show the soldiers our passports. Maram keeps my phone and her passport. "I will tell them about us, that we are going to the Rafah border crossing and that our son is an American citizen," I say. But I have taken only a few steps when a soldier orders me to freeze. I am so scared that I forget to look back at Mostafa. I can hear him crying.

I join a long queue of young men on their knees. A soldier is ordering two elderly women, who seem to be waiting for men who have been detained, to keep walking. "If you don't move, we will shoot you," the soldier says. Behind me, a young man is sobbing. "Why have they picked me? I'm a farmer," he says. Don't worry, I tell him. They will question and then release us.

After half an hour, I hear my full name, twice: "Mosab Mostafa Hasan Abu Toha." I'm puzzled. I didn't show anyone my ID when I was pulled out of line. How do they know my name?

I walk toward an Israeli jeep. The barrel of a gun points at me. When I am asked for my ID number, I recite it as loud as I can.

"OK, sit next to the others."

About ten of us are now kneeling in the sand. I can see piles of money, cigarettes, mobile phones, watches, and wallets. I recognize a man from my neighborhood, who is slightly younger than my father. "The most important thing is that they don't take us as human shields for their tanks," he says. This possibility never crossed my mind, and my terror grows.

We are led, two by two, to a clearing near a wall. A soldier with a megaphone tells us to undress; two others point guns at us. I strip down to my boxer shorts, and so does the young man next to me.

The soldier orders us to continue. We look at each other, shocked. I think I see movement from one of the armed soldiers, and fear for my life. We take off our boxer shorts.

"Turn around!"

This is the first time in my life that strangers have looked at me naked. They speak in Hebrew and seem cheerful. Are they joking about the hair on my body? Maybe they can see the scars where shrapnel sliced into my forehead and neck when I was sixteen. A soldier asks about my travel documents. "These are our passports," I say, shivering. "We are heading to the Rafah border crossing."

"Shut up, you son of a bitch."

I am allowed to put on my clothes, but not my jacket. They take my wallet and tie my hands behind my back with plastic handcuffs. One of the soldiers comments on my UNRWA employee card. "I'm a teacher," I tell him. He curses at me again.

The soldiers blindfold me and attach a numbered bracelet to one wrist. I wonder how Israelis would feel if they were known by a number. Then someone grabs the back of my neck and shoves me forward, as though we are sheep on our way to be slaughtered. I keep asking for someone to talk to, but no one responds. The earth is muddy and cold and strewn with rubble.

I am pushed onto my knees, and then made to stand, and then ordered to kneel again. Soldiers keep asking in Arabic, "What's your name? What's your ID number?"

A man addresses me in English. "You are an activist. With Hamas, right?"

"Me? I swear, no. I stopped going to the mosque in 2010, when I started attending university. I spent the last four years in the United States and earned my MFA in creative writing from Syracuse University."

He seems surprised.

"Some Hamas members we arrested admitted you are a Hamas member."

"They are lying." I ask for proof.

He slaps me across the face. "*You* get me proof that you are not Hamas!"

Everything around me is dark and frightening. I ask myself, how can a person get proof of something that he is not? Then I am walked aggressively forward again. What did I do? Where will they take us?

I am told to remove my shoes, and a group of us are led somewhere else. Cold rain and wind strike our backs.

"You raped our girls," someone says. "You killed our kids." He slaps our necks and kicks our backs with heavy boots. In the distance, we can hear artillery fire slicing through the air.

One by one, we are forced into a truck. Someone who is not moving lands on my lap. I fear that a soldier has thrown a corpse onto me, as a form of torture, but I am scared to speak. I whisper, "Are you alive?"

"Yes, man," the person says, and I sigh with relief.

When the truck stops, we hear what sound like gunshots. I no longer feel my body. The soldiers give off a smell that reminds me of coffins. I find myself wishing that a heart attack would kill me.

At our next stop, we kneel outside again. I start to wonder whether the Israeli military is showing us off. When a young man next to me cries, "No Hamas, no Hamas!," I hear kicks until he falls silent.

Another man, maybe talking to himself, says quietly, "I need to be with my daughter and pregnant wife. Please."

My eyes fill with tears. I imagine Maram and our kids on the other side of the checkpoint. They don't have blankets or even enough clothes. I can hear female soldiers, chatting and laughing.

Suddenly, someone kicks me in the stomach. I fly back and hit the ground, breathless. I cry out in Arabic for my mother.

I am forced back onto my knees. There is no time to feel scared. A boot kicks me in the nose and mouth. I feel that I am almost finished, but the nightmare is not over.

Back in the truck, my body hurts so much that I wish I had no hands or shoulders. After what feels like ninety minutes of driving, we are taken off the truck and shoved down some stairs. A soldier cuts my plastic handcuffs. "Both hands on the fence," he says.

This time, the soldier ties my hands in the front. A sigh of relief. I am escorted about fifteen meters. Finally, someone speaks to me in what sounds like native Palestinian Arabic. He seems to be my father's age.

At first, I hate this man. I think he is a collaborator. But later I hear him described as a *shawish*—a detainee like us, with little choice but to work for his jailers. "Let me help you," he says.

The *shawish* dresses me in new clothes and walks me inside the fence. When I raise my blindfolded head, I get blurry glimpses of a corrugated metal roof. We are in some kind of detention center; soldiers walk around, watching us. The *shawish* unrolls what looks like a yoga mat and covers me with a thin blanket. I place my bound hands behind my head, as a pillow. My arms sear with pain, but my body slowly warms. This is the end of day one.

For years, I have dreamed of looking out the window of a plane and seeing my home from above. In my adult life, I have never seen a civilian flight over Gaza. I have seen only warplanes and drones. Israel bombed Gaza's international airport in the early 2000s, during the Second Intifada, and it has not operated since.

Most of my friends have never left Gaza. But in recent years, as they have struggled to find jobs and feed families, they have asked, *how long should I wait?* Some have immigrated to Turkey, and then to Europe. Some envy my three trips to the United States. Each time I have returned, with photos of unfamiliar cities and trees and snow, people have called me "the American," and asked me why I came back. There is nothing in Gaza, they say. I always tell them that I want to be with my family and my neighbors. I have my house and my teaching job and my books. I can play soccer with my friends and go out to eat. Why would I leave Gaza?

We wake to the sound of a soldier shouting into a megaphone. The *shawish* makes sure everyone is kneeling on the floor. He has told us that we are in a place called Be'er Sheva, in the Negev Desert. This is my first time in Israel.

The youngest of us, whose voice I recognize from the line, suddenly screams out that he is innocent. "I need to see my mother," he says. My feet start to feel numb.

I hear shouting and beating. "OK, OK, I will shut up," he says. "But please send me back." More beating follows.

The person next to me asks the *shawish* for water. "No water yet," the *shawish* says. He sounds frustrated, and I sympathize with him. More than a hundred detainees depend on him. When he takes me to the toilet, for the first time since the previous morning, he has to help me open the door and position me to urinate. The stench is very strong.

Breakfast is a small piece of bread, some yogurt, and a slosh of water poured directly into our mouths. I am not hungry, not even for my mother's birthday cake. When I return to the toilet, around noon, the *shawish* tells me that there is no toilet paper or water to wash myself.

Later, a soldier tells the *shawish* that we will be going to see a doctor. I sense relief in the room.

"I will tell him about my diabetes."

"Yes, and I will tell him about my bladder problem."

I will tell him about the pain in my nose, upper jaw, and right ear, where I had surgery a few years ago. Since I was kicked in the face, my hearing is weaker than before.

We kneel outside, with our hands on the back of the person in front of us. Wind strikes us; stones dig into our knees. We are put in a bus and a soldier pushes my head down, even though I can't see anything. Maybe they don't want to look at our faces.

When we exit the truck and my name is called, I am temporarily given my ID card. I feel a prick of hope. Maybe they are going to release us.

Inside a building, my blindfold is pulled off. A soldier is aiming an M-16 at my head. Another soldier, behind a computer, asks questions and takes a photo of me. Another numbered badge is fastened to my left arm. Then I see the doctor, who asks whether I suffer from chronic diseases or feel sick. He does not seem interested in my pain.

Back at the detention center, blindfolded again, we kneel painfully for hours. I try to sleep. A man moans nearby; another is hopeful that he will get to go back to the doctor. Late in the evening, a soldier calls my name. The *shawish* leads me to the gate, and a jeep comes to take me away.

I am tied to a chair in a small room. An Israeli officer, Captain T., comes in and asks, "*Marhaba, keefak?*" This is Arabic for "Hello, how are you?"

I am very sad because of everything that has been done to me, I tell him.

"Don't be sad," he says. "We will talk."

The captain leaves the room and comes back with coffee. A soldier unties my right arm, so I can hold my cup.

I will tell him everything about me, I say, including where I was on October 7, but I want him to answer one question.

"Sure. I'm listening."

Will he release me if there is nothing on me?

He promises that he will.

He takes notes as I tell him about my trips to the United States, my poetry book, and my English students. I tell him that on the morning of October 7, when Hamas began to launch rockets at Israel, I was wearing some new clothes, and my wife was taking a photo of me. The sound of rockets made Yaffa cry, so I showed her some YouTube videos on my phone. My father and brothers were on different floors of the house, and we started to shout a conversation out the windows. What's happening? Is this some kind of test?

On Telegram, we started to find videos of Hamas fighters inside Israel with their jeeps and motorcycles, encircling houses and shooting Israeli soldiers. In the beginning, some Gazans seemed excited and happy about the attack. But many of us were perplexed and scared. Although Gaza has been devastated by the Israeli occupation, I could not justify the atrocities committed against Israeli civilians. There is no reason to kill anyone like that. I also knew Israel would respond. Hamas had never done something like this before, and I feared that Israeli retaliation would be unprecedented, too.

Captain T. asks me two questions. First, do I know of any Hamas tunnels or plans for ambushes?

I spent most of the past four years in the United States, I say. I spend my time teaching, reading, writing, and playing soccer. I don't know these things, and I'm not involved with Hamas.

Then Captain T. asks me the names and ages of my family members. Before I leave, he tells me that he hails from a

family of Moroccan Jews. There are many shared things
between us, he says. I nod and smile, trying to believe that he
means what he says.

I ask him what will happen to me. They will look into what
I have told him, he says. It may take several days.

"And then?"

"We will either imprison or release you."

I am on a bed, shackled and waiting to go back to the
detention center. Someone comes to take me away but then
stops and has a conversation with someone else. They leave
me for a while, and I fall asleep to the sound of Hebrew
music. I like the singer's voice.

When I wake, a soldier says something in English that I
cannot believe.

"We are sorry about the mistake. You are going home."

"Are you serious?"

Silence.

"I will go back to Gaza and be with my family?"

"Why wouldn't I be serious?"

Another voice chimes in: "Isn't this the writer?"

Back at the detention center, as I fall asleep, I think about
the words "We are sorry about the mistake." I wonder how
many mistakes the Israeli Army has made, and whether they
will say sorry to anyone else.

On Tuesday, about two days after I left the school, the man
with the megaphone teaches us how to say good morning in
Hebrew. "*Boker Tov*, Captain," we say in unison. Some new
detainees have arrived in an enclosure nearby, and the soldiers
overseeing them seem to be having fun. They sing part of an

Arabic children's song, "Oh, my sheep!," and order the detainees to say "Baa" in response.

About an hour later, a soldier calls out my name and orders me to stand near the gate. The *shawish* warns me that they might interrogate me and beat me again. "Be strong and don't lie," he says. I feel a surge of panic.

After an hour, some soldiers approach. One has my ID, and another drops a pair of slippers for me and tells me to walk. Then one of them says, "Release!"

I am so overjoyed that I thank him. I think about my wife and children. I hope that my parents and siblings are alive.

I spend about two hours at the place where I was interrogated, with the Hebrew music. I am given some food and water, but the soldiers never find my family's passports. I climb into a jeep, surrounded by soldiers. After two hours, I can see around my blindfold that we are getting close to Gaza.

The soldiers get out, smoke, and return fully armed, wearing their vests and helmets. I am thinking about the man I recognized in line, and what he said about human shields. I am starting to wish that I could go back to the detention center when they give me my ID card.

Standing against a wall, I tell the closest soldier that I am scared.

"Do not feel scared. You will leave soon."

My handcuffs are cut, and the blindfold is removed. I see the place where I had to take my clothes off. When I see new detainees waiting there, sadness overwhelms me.

I walk fast. Back at the checkpoint, in a big pile of belongings, I find my handbag, but not Yazzan's backpack, where we stuffed our children's winter clothes. A soldier shouts angrily at me. "I was just released," I say.

Back on Salah al-Din Road, dozens of people are waiting. A crying mother asks if I have seen her son. "He was kidnapped on Monday," she says. It is Tuesday. I have not seen him.

I have no money and no phone, but a kind driver offers to drop me off in the southern city of Deir al-Balah. I know that my wife's relatives have taken refuge there, and Maram probably would have joined them with the kids. As the man drives, I keep asking where we are, and he recites the names of refugee camps: Al-Nuseirat, Al-Bureij, Al-Maghazi.

In Deir al-Balah, I ask some young people, who are standing outside a bank, using its Wi-Fi, whether they know anyone from my hometown. One of them points me toward a school.

I take off my slippers and start to run. Passersby are staring, but I don't care. Suddenly, I spot an old friend, Mahdi, who once was the goalkeeper on my soccer team. "Mahdi! I'm lost—help me."

"Mosab!" We hug each other.

"Your wife and kids are at the school next to the college," he says. "Just turn left and walk for about two hundred meters."

I cry as I run. Just when I start to worry that I have lost my way, I hear Yaffa's voice. "Daddy!" She is the first piece of my puzzle. She seems healthy and is eating an orange. When I ask where the rest of the family is, she takes my hand and pulls me as if I were a child.

Maram's uncle Sari rushes off to find Maram. He does not tell her that I have arrived, only that she should return to the school for dinner. When she sees me, she looks like she might collapse, and I run toward her.

I learn from Maram how lucky I was. She used my phone to inform friends around the world, who demanded my safe release. I think about the hundreds or thousands of Palestinians, many of them likely more talented than me, who were taken from the checkpoint. Their friends could not help them.

At my friend's apartment in Cairo, I see flowers that my parents grew in northern Gaza.

The next day, Wednesday, I go to the hospital to have my injuries examined and see patients and corpses everywhere—in the corridors, on the steps, on desks. I manage to get an X-ray, but there are no results: The doctor's computer isn't working. I leave with a prescription for painkillers.

That Friday, a temporary ceasefire begins. Two of my wife's uncles try to go north, only to return an hour later. They say that Israeli snipers have shot and killed two people. At the souk, clothing costs more than ever. I wait five hours at an UNRWA aid center in the hope of receiving some flour, without success. A line to refill gas cannisters seems about a kilometer long.

As soon as the ceasefire ends, about 700 Palestinians are killed in twenty-four hours. Until recently, the south has been comparatively safe, but now we hear bombs not far away.

Then the US Embassy in Jerusalem calls, advising us to head to the Rafah border crossing.

I struggle to find us a ride. The journey is about twenty kilometers, and the first two drivers we ask are scared. Israeli forces have isolated Rafah from the nearby city of Khan Younis. After a few calls, Maram's cousin, a taxi driver, agrees to take us.

At the crossing, we wait with hundreds of Gazans for four hours. I have my ID, which lists my children's names, but only Maram has her passport. I worry that we don't have the right documents to get through the crossing. But at 7:00 p.m. officials wave us through the gate, and we join a crowd of exhausted families in the Egyptian travelers' hall. I feel as though I have been cured. The American Embassy gives us an emergency passport for Mostafa, and the Palestinian Embassy gives us single-use travel documents. Then a minibus takes us to Cairo.

In "A State of Siege," the Palestinian poet Mahmoud Darwish writes something that is difficult to translate. "We do what jobless people do," he says. "We raise hope." The verb *nurabi*, meaning to raise or to rear, is what a parent does for a child, or what a farmer does for crops. "Hope" is a difficult word for Palestinians. It is not something that others give us but something that we must cultivate and care for on our own. We have to help hope grow.

I hope that when the war ends, I can go back to Gaza, to help rebuild my family home and fill it with books. That one day all Israelis can see us as their equals—as people who need to live on our own land, in safety and prosperity, and build a future. That my dream of seeing Gaza from a plane can become a reality, and that my home can grow many more dreams. It's true that there are many things to criticize Palestinians for. We are divided. We suffer from corruption. Many of our leaders do not represent us. Some people are violent. But, in the end, we Palestinians share at least one thing with Israelis. We must have our own country—or live together in one country, in which Palestinians have full and equal rights. We should have our own airport and seaport and economy—what any other country has.

An Egyptian friend welcomes us to Cairo. She lives in the Zamalek neighborhood, on an island in the Nile. When I visit her garden, I see flowers that my parents grew in Beit Lahia. On her shelves, I see books that I left behind, under the rubble. When I tell her that her house reminds me of home, she begins to cry.

Later, I find an article in the Israeli newspaper *Haaretz* about a detention center in Be'er Sheva. It describes the same conditions that I experienced and says that several detainees have died in Israeli custody. When the Israeli Army is reached for comment about my story, a spokesperson says, "Detainees are treated in line with international standards, including necessary checks for concealed weapons. The IDF prioritizes detainee dignity and will review any deviations from protocols." The spokesperson does not comment on detainee deaths.

On Telegram, I find a video of Khalifa Bin Zayed Elementary, an UNRWA school that Yazzan, Yaffa, and I all attended. Two of Maram's uncles, Naseem and Ramadan, who were born deaf and mute, have been sheltering there with their families. When the kids hear the video, they drop their toys and join me. "There is my classroom," Yaffa says. She started first grade a few weeks ago. Yazzan sees his classroom, too. In the video, the school is on fire.

I learn from a relative that the men in the school were taken to a hospital, stripped, and interrogated by Israeli forces. Afterward, Naseem and Ramadan went looking for their children. My relative says that, near the entrance to the school, a sniper shot them both, killing Naseem.

Naseem's younger brother Sari, whom I saw only days ago, sends me a photo of Naseem, wearing a white doctor's uniform stained with his blood. "These were the only clothes they could find at the hospital," Sari tells me on WhatsApp. Maram sits next to me, weeping.

The next day, Maram is cooking *maqluba*, a dish of rice, meat, and vegetables, which I have not eaten for two months. I am savoring the smell of potatoes and tomatoes when I get a call from a private number.

"Hello, Mosab. How are you?"

It is my father-in-law, Jaleel. At the sound of his voice, Maram's eyes brim with tears. He tells us that everything is fine, even though we know that this can't possibly be true. Then her mother comes to the phone.

"I'm sorry for our loss, Mum," Maram says. I hear her mother sob.

"Mum, are you taking your medicine?"

"Don't worry about me," she says. We never stop worrying about them.

I do not know whether our journey will end in Egypt or continue to the United States. I only know that my children need to have a childhood. They need to travel, and be educated, and live a life that is different from mine.

I have come to Egypt with only one book, a worn-out copy of my poetry collection. Since I last read it, I have lived a lot of new poems, which I still have to write. After weeks of typing on my phone, in streets and in schools, I am not used to opening my laptop without worrying about when I can charge it. I am not used to being able to close the door. But one morning I sit at my friend's beautiful wooden desk, in a room full of light, and write a poem. It is addressed to my mother. I hope that the next time we speak I can read it to her.

# 8

# On Teaching in Gaza

## *Eman Basher*

I used to be an English teacher. My classroom walls seemed to breathe with the wind, and the light depended on the mercy of the sun; a very eco-friendly setup, if you think about it. Who needs electricity when the sun graciously decides to show up for class?

For eight years, I taught in Beit Hanoun Prep School for young girls; a place where optimism stubbornly thrived in conditions that would make even the most dedicated teachers elsewhere quit by lunchtime. Beit Hanoun, the closest city to the Israeli settlements in Sderot, was the first to face evacuations during escalations. The village I worked in was often referred to as "Bora," meaning "wasteland" in English, a grim nickname earned from the relentless bombing by Israeli warplanes.

In this battered corner of the world, poetry, stories, and literature were the tools we used to carve out moments of imagination in a world that often felt like it had none to spare. I introduced my ninth graders to Maya Angelou, Mahmoud Darwish, and Langston Hughes. And let me tell you, when a fourteen-year-old in a war zone starts dissecting the nuances of "I Know Why the Caged Bird Sings," you can't help but marvel at the irony. These weren't just students; they were young women whose lives were already laced with feminist resistance. They didn't need lectures on empowerment; they lived it every day, walking miles to school, clinging to their books as though education could physically shield them from the chaos outside. And maybe it did, if only for a few hours. They wrote stories in which women were heroes and poems that raged against injustice, all while the world shrugged and called them statistics. In that drafty little classroom, with sunlight doubling as our electricity, these girls found power in words, even when the world seemed hell-bent on silencing them. It was absurd, really, that the most fragile place could also be the strongest, but that's Gaza for you—a place where hope is the ultimate act of defiance.

In Gaza, education has long been a beacon of hope amid adversity. For many girls, attending school is a cherished opportunity, even when resources are scarce. Classrooms often lack basic amenities; it's not uncommon for students to sit on the floor due to a shortage of chairs. Despite these challenges, these young women engage passionately in their studies, including lessons on feminism and empowerment. My girls came to school without lunch boxes, without raincoats, and on foot. To a class that did not have enough chairs and tables and often leaked on heavy rainy days. Yet, they came. And kept coming. And insisted on coming. I used to look at their combed ponytails and pretty hairclips and see them as tiny freedom fighters, little super women who do not have the luxury of three meals a day yet would always come to school with combed hair and clean, ironed clothes. And I wanted to offer them the fine education they deserved. I would give my life if I could. They put every effort into learning so that they might have a future. Yet, the world offered nothing in return.

However, after the genocide began, even this fragile system crumbled. Schools have been reduced to rubble, with over 200 facilities targeted by airstrikes. The tiny joy of learning is replaced by the fear of death. The absence of basic necessities—like water and hygiene products—has forced young girls into indignities unimaginable in classrooms elsewhere. Dreams once nurtured by education are now buried under debris and stolen by violence. The contrast is stark: what was once a glimmer of hope is now a sobering reminder of what has been lost—a generation deprived not only of education but of the dignity and safety that should come with it.

The recent escalation of violence has made their already difficult lives unbearable. With infrastructure destroyed, severe water shortages have forced some girls to cut their hair just to maintain basic hygiene. The lack of sanitary products has left them using improvised materials, stripping away the dignity they deserve. These deeply personal struggles are rarely noticed by the global community, overshadowed by the broader narrative of conflict. How can these girls be expected to focus on their education when the world reduces them to mere objects of control; when something as personal as their hair is stripped away without care for their dignity, when their schools are targets instead of sanctuaries, and when their humanity is overlooked entirely? In such a reality, pursuing education becomes more than learning; it becomes a fight to hold on to their identity.

As I write this, I stand in the Arts and Sciences building at the University of Wyoming, where the hum of electricity is constant, and the Wi-Fi buzzes louder than my own thoughts. In September 2024, my professor invited me to be a guest speaker in one of his classes to talk about Palestine. Sensing my apprehension, he reassured me, saying, "They know nothing about Gaza, and that's exactly why you should start telling your stories." The absurdity of it all struck me: I survived a genocide funded and supported by the United States last February, and here I am, in September of the same year, preparing to lecture American students about the very country complicit in it. It's hard to think about standing in front of a classroom and explaining the reality of Gaza to students whose biggest worries might be grades or deadlines—when my own students back home, the ones I taught in Gaza, can barely dream of such normalcy.

How do I convey that to these American students, whose world feels so far removed from the one my students live in? How do I even begin to tell them about a place where every child is a walking testament to resilience but also a reminder of the world's failure? And then there's me; someone who taught in Gaza but now stands in this surreal position, trying to bridge two worlds that should never have collided this way. It feels obscene, trying to translate devastation into digestible lessons, as if it's just another academic exercise. How do I put into words the reality that while I speak, my mom lives in a tent and my students back home write essays about survival instead of Shakespeare?

I can't help but feel the absurdity, the heaviness of the irony: to be asked to educate about Gaza while knowing the very education my own students deserve is stolen from them every day. Words can't feed the hungry or stop Israeli tanks from crushing the bodies of our children. I feel like I'm living in a twisted form of dark comedy, where the punchline is always despair. Words are supposed to matter, as in satire or political commentary. Think of how dark comedy uses humor to navigate the unbearable—yet even humor feels hollow now. There are no punchlines that can soften this pain, no clever lines that can undo the damage. It's like using poetry to rebuild bombed-out buildings or trying to wield sarcasm as a shield against missiles. The absurdity of it all is over-whelming. Attending my students' funerals instead of their graduation parties is overwhelming.

In Jenan's story, there wasn't even a funeral to attend. Jenan Al-Masri, an eighth grader who embodied everything education is supposed to nurture: hope, ambition, and the courage to dream beyond the confines of oppression. Before the genocide began, Jenan had been chosen to give a speech about peace. Peace. The concept she believed in, the word she was preparing to speak to the world, was stolen from her by the very forces she hoped to see subdued. On October 21, 2023, an Israeli airstrike killed Jenan, her parents, and two sisters, leaving behind a single surviving brother to mourn them. She never got to deliver her speech. The irony is gut-wrenching—she dreamed of standing before others to advocate for peace, but her life was extinguished by the violence she sought to end.

Jenan's face haunts me daily. It mirrors the stolen dreams of so many students I've taught, students who've scribbled their hopes in notebooks as bombs fell outside their windows. I think of Jenan and wonder: What if the world had listened? What if the world had cared enough to see her not as a statistic but as a child; a poet of peace, a future doctor, artist, or teacher? This question challenges the tendency to reduce human lives to numbers, ignoring the extraordinary potential that thrives in the most unlikely places. Gaza's education system is a testament to this potential, achieving remarkable success against all odds.

Despite being under blockade, facing constant attacks, and suffering from severe shortages of resources, Gaza boasts a literacy rate of over 97 percent, one of the highest in the Arab world. Classrooms are overcrowded, power outages are frequent, and teachers often work without pay. Yet, students excel in national and international exams, earning scholarships to universities around the globe. In recent years, Gazan graduates have entered fields from medicine and engineering to law, art, and education, proving that even in a place ravaged by war, knowledge can flourish.

The girls I taught in Beit Hanoun Prep School were part of this legacy of determination. They clung to their books with a conviction that education could change their futures.

Farah Nusair had an insatiable curiosity for literature,

often staying after class to ask about the hidden meanings behind poems. She once wrote a breathtaking essay about hope, weaving metaphors that felt far beyond her years. Malak Kafarneh possessed an analytical mind and a love for problem-solving. Her favorite moments were when she could break down complex ideas in science lessons and explain them to her classmates, her face lighting up with every "aha" moment. Doaa Masri was a budding artist. Her notebooks were filled with intricate sketches, and she had a remarkable talent for turning historical lessons into vivid illustrations, helping her peers see history through her eyes. Lena Ashour had a natural gift for storytelling. She loved creative writing assignments, crafting tales that transported her classmates to other worlds, her vivid imagination painting images more colorful than reality. Dima Nusair had a sharp wit and a talent for debate. She would challenge ideas in class, always with respect but with a hunger to explore perspectives that others hadn't considered. Jenan Al-Masri was a quiet yet brilliant presence. She had a love for numbers and excelled in mathematics, often solving problems faster than anyone in the room, her shy smile revealing her pride when others clapped for her. Each of these girls had a spark that promised a future filled with possibility, a reminder of the infinite potential that was so cruelly extinguished.

The tragedy is not just in the lives lost but in the futures stolen. These children were dreamers and doers, equipped with resilience to turn education into opportunity. What could they have become if the world had cared enough to protect their right to dream? If Gaza's education system can produce this brilliance in the face of unimaginable adversity, imagine what could be possible if these children had the same resources and freedoms as their peers elsewhere.

More than 50,000 children have been killed or injured in the Gaza Strip since October 7, 2023, according to UNICEF, amid widespread airstrikes by the Israeli military. Hundreds more are reported missing and may be trapped under the rubble. These statistics represent not just numbers but the silenced voices of students who once aspired to learn and lead. Their stories underscore the urgent need for global attention and action to protect the fundamental right to education, even in the most challenging circumstances.

Nothing prepares a teacher to attend the funerals of her students, one after another. There's no greater sense of defeat than standing before a class of young women, speaking of hope and peace, filling them with the belief that they are the promise of a better world—only for that world to hand them a tent the next day.

Maybe that's the cruelest lesson of all—that I'm here, lecturing about resilience when the world did everything in its power to crush it.

# 9

# Ecocide in Palestine

## *Nina Lakhani*

"Among all the problems facing Palestinians, climate change is the most immediate and certain. We have been trying to do our part to mitigate and adapt but as a country under occupation it is already very hard to implement our policies as all our projects—agriculture, water harvesting, renewables—have to be first approved by Israel, and can be destroyed or stopped at any point."

"That was our reality before October 7, before the chemicals and carbon emissions from the bombs. Now Israel is destroying Gaza. How will we implement climate adaptation plans when there is nothing left? How can we talk about climate justice while our people and land are being destroyed?"

I first met Hadeel Ikhmais in December 2023 as the twenty-eighth annual UN climate summit was wrapping up in Dubai. Hadeel heads the Climate Change Unit at the Palestinian Environmental Quality Authority (EQA) in Ramallah, leading the State of Palestine's efforts to adapt to worsening drought, floods, extreme heat, dust, and rising sea level—and transition away from fossil fuels.

As negotiations wrapped up at Cop28, the United States—by far the biggest supplier of military equipment to Israel—vetoed a UN Security Council vote calling for a ceasefire in Gaza. The vote took place when Israeli aerial bombardments had already destroyed or damaged several of Gaza's water and sanitation plants, as well as crops, orchards, greenhouses, and solar energy projects that Hadeel and her colleagues had worked for years to secure. Some 18,000 people had already been killed and tens of thousands were injured or missing under the rubble.

Since then, weapon sales have soared and the scale and speed of the destruction of Gaza's built and natural environment has been unprecedented and cataclysmic. By the end of June 2024, approximately 83 percent of all plant life and 70 percent of farmland had been destroyed in Gaza, according to Forensic Architecture (FA). A UN satellite assessment found at least 163,778 schools, clinics, shops, mosques, bridges, and other structures in the Gaza Strip had been damaged or destroyed by early September 2024. To put the destruction into perspective, in less than a year Israel had bombed around four times the total number of buildings in Manhattan. According to another UN study, the relentless bombardment has left an estimated 42 million tons of debris piled where Palestinians once lived, worked, prayed, and played—an inconceivable quantity of concrete mixed in with toxic waste, unexploded munitions, and human remains that will poison the air, land, and water for Palestinians for decades to come. Reconstructing Gaza from the rubble will generate roughly the same quantity of greenhouse gases emitted by Uganda in 2023, a country of 49 million people.

The scale and pattern of Israeli attacks suggest Israel has systematically targeted civilian infrastructure, agriculture and other food sources, water, and sanitation—destroying critical infrastructure and other objects indispensable to the survival of the Palestinians in Gaza. By June 2024, not a single wastewater treatment facility was operational in Gaza, and waterborne diseases such as cholera, Hepatitis A, and dysentery were rife as sewage spewed into the sea, streets, and internally displaced persons (IDP) camps. An estimated 5.4 percent of all Gazans had been killed by bombs, disease, and hunger within a year.

"They have destroyed what makes us human and targeted every aspect of Palestinian life so there is nowhere for us to live or work or feed ourselves," said Hadeel on a video call in November 2024.

Israel's destruction of Gaza bears the hallmark of scorched-earth operations carried out by US-backed and US-funded right-wing dictatorships in Central America during the 1980s. In Guatemala, the genocide of the Ixil Mayans in the western highlands involved executions, sexual violence, and the razing of villages, fields, and forests. "This destruction rendered the area uninhabitable and forced survivors to displace to areas under the control of the government. Altering the environment was key to the destruction of Ixil culture," concluded the research and visual investigations group Forensic Architecture. The Guatemalan military dictatorship classified Indigenous communities living in areas where guerilla fighters were operating as communist enemies. Scorched-earth tactics were coded as "clean-up" operations and "sweeps," according to classified military documents obtained years after the massacres by the National Security Archive.

On October 12, 2023, Israeli President Isaac Herzog held all Palestinians in Gaza responsible for the attack by Hamas five days earlier: "It's an entire nation out there that is responsible. It's not true this rhetoric about civilians not aware, not involved . . . we will fight until we break their backbone." In a video posted online on November 4, 2023, from inside Gaza, Brigadier General Yogev Bar Sheshet said: "Whoever returns here, if they return here after, will find scorched earth. No houses, no agriculture, no nothing. They have no future." The subsequent destruction of Gaza suggests that the Israeli regime, like the Guatemalan dictatorship, understood that to destroy the people, you must destroy their land, homes, animals, their whole living ecosystem—and crucially, *their hope of return*.

"Gaza is more than a place; it is the beating heart of our identity, a symbol of unbreakable will," said Adham Madi, a twenty-eight-year-old lawyer from Gaza City, who messaged me from an IDP camp in the city of Deir al-Balah. "For us, the land is sacred, and Gaza is a living testament to the unyielding spirit of Palestine." Adham sent me a photo of his apartment building in Gaza City's Al-Ramal neighborhood, after it had been razed by an Israeli bomb in December 2023. Still, he hopes to return and rebuild one day. "Every inch of this land holds the stories of loved ones lost, homes destroyed, and dreams deferred. It is the place where our ancestors are buried, where our children cling to hope amid the devastation. The connection is one of survival and resistance, of love and longing."

## *No Water*

On October 9, 2023, the Israeli defense minister, Yoav Gallant, ordered a complete siege on the Gaza Strip. "There will be no electricity, no food, no fuel, everything is closed." Shortly after, energy minister Israel Katz shut off fuel, electricity, and water supplies. After just three days of Israeli airstrikes, at least six water wells, three water pumping stations, one water reservoir, and one desalination plant serving over 1.1 million people had been damaged. Israel had also shut off water from its state-owned company, which supplied 12 percent of Gaza.

Deliberately depriving citizens of objects indispensable to their survival—such as water, food, energy, and humanitarian aid—is a violation of international law, as is collective punishment. Undeterred, Israel weaponized water in a myriad of ways. In November 2023, Israeli airstrikes destroyed the solar panels and other essential infrastructure at the German-financed Gaza Central wastewater treatment plant, which treated the sewage of half the population. A few weeks later, the military began pumping seawater into Hamas's tunnel network in an effort to destroy their clandestine transport and communications system. A hydrologist told the *Guardian* that this risked "ruining the basic conditions for life in Gaza"—an element of the crime of genocide.

On February 8, 2024, Israeli snipers shot dead eight Palestinians who were filling water near Nasser Hospital, west of Khan Younis.

The attacks on water and sanitation infrastructure continued despite mounting evidence that Palestinian children were dying from waterborne diseases. In July 2024, Salama Shurrab, head of the water networks at Khan Younis municipality, told Reuters that soldiers had destroyed thirty water wells over the course of ten days in the southern towns of Rafah and Khan Younis. In addition, a reservoir serving thousands of internally displaced people seeking refuge around Rafah was blown up. A soldier posted a video of the explosion on YouTube with the caption, "Destruction of the Tel Sultan water reservoir in honour of Shabbat."

"In the past, water shortages were not a major concern as almost every home or plot of land had some solar panels to pump underground water. But now, with the destruction of wells and the solar panels that powered them, the situation has become dire," said Akram Basel, twenty-nine, a displaced structural engineer from Gaza City, who has worked on water and sanitation projects.

Israel also severely restricted humanitarian aid including potable water, desalination units and pipes, and other parts required to fix destroyed water and infrastructure—in violation of the ruling on January 26, 2024, by the International Court of Justice (ICJ) on the genocide case brought by South Africa.

All in all, the impact of Israel's war on water has been catastrophic on public health. A study by Oxfam found that people in Gaza had only 4.74 liters of water per person per day for all uses including drinking, cooking, and bathing—a staggering 94 percent reduction in the amount of water available before Israel's war on Gaza. The internationally accepted minimum in extreme emergencies such as in the wake of an earthquake or climate disaster is 15 liters of water per person per day. By mid-2024, more than a quarter of the population had fallen seriously ill from preventable waterborne diseases.

"At the beginning of the war, senior Israeli Army commanders and government ministers made explicit their determination to cut off food, medicine, and water to the population of the Gaza Strip. And they have done so in a systematic way," said Pedro Arrojo-Agudo, the UN special rapporteur on the human rights to safe drinking water and sanitation. "It is very clear to me that cutting off access to water is not just a crime against humanity, it's part of a genocidal and ethnic cleansing strategy being carried out not just now in Gaza—but also in the West Bank for decades."

The evidence suggests that Israel's assault on Palestinian water supplies has been a key element of its decades-long apartheid regime, used to create intolerable, unlivable conditions and the expansion of illegal settlements across the occupied territories. According to the Pacific Institute's water violence tracker, in one case in June 2022, the Israeli Army destroyed a Palestinian-owned water well dug on municipal land that was used for the entire town of Beit Lid, east of Tulkarm, filling it with rocks and concrete. (In November 2023, settlers protected by the army returned to destroy the main water line supplying the entire town.) In September

2022, Israeli settlers and military forces razed Palestinian-owned land and uprooted fifty olive trees near Zawiya village in Salfit, West Bank, to set up water networks for an illegal settlement. Overall, Israel attacked Palestinian water sources at least sixty-six times between January 2022 and mid-2023—more water-related violence than was inflicted on Ukraine by Russia over the same period.

The water-related violence—and land grabs—have accelerated since October 7. In one incident on December 24, Israeli settler rioters destroyed water containers, irrigation lines, and sixty olive trees on Palestinian-owned lands in Qitaa Kamel in Jalud, Nablus, West Bank. "Using water as a weapon is not an accident," said Arrojo-Agudo. "It is a very important element of systematically ethnically cleansing the territories and making life impossible for the Palestinian people."

### Starvation

In February 2024, Michael Fakhri, the UN special rapporteur on the right to food, said that Palestinians in Gaza were being intentionally starved and the State of Israel—and individuals—should be held culpable for war crimes and genocide. "We have never seen a civilian population made to go so hungry so quickly and so completely. Israel is not just targeting civilians, it is trying to damn the future of the Palestinian people by harming their children."

It took nine more months for the International Criminal Court (ICC) to issue arrest warrants for Israeli Prime

Minister Benjamin Netanyahu and the recently fired defense minister, Yoav Gallant, for alleged war crimes and crimes against humanity—including the use of starvation as a method of warfare. The judges said there were reasonable grounds to believe Netanyahu and Gallant jointly with others "intentionally and knowingly" deprived Palestinians civilians of objects indispensable to their survival—with the intention of bringing about the destruction of part of the population in Gaza.

As the cogs of international justice chugged along, more than 62,000 people, mostly young children, likely died of starvation and its complications in Gaza between October 7, 2023, and September 30, 2024, according to a report by ninety-nine American medical professionals of the Integrated Food Security Phase Classification (IPC), who returned from Gaza with harrowing eyewitness accounts. "Every day I saw babies die. They had been born healthy. Their mothers were so malnourished that they could not breastfeed, and we lacked formula or clean water to feed them, so they starved," wrote Asma Taha, a pediatric nurse practitioner, in a letter sent to the Biden administration.

Israel's war on Gaza made 95 percent or 2.15 million Palestinians in Gaza go hungry within a year—a period in which the United States spent at least $22.76 billion on military aid to Israel and related US operations in the region. Around 90 percent of the population has been forcibly displaced, repeatedly fleeing tanks and bombs while dehydrated and starving.

The ICC charges focus on the deliberate blocking of

humanitarian aid. But Israel has also deliberately bombed and razed crops, greenhouses, orchards, fisheries, and other food sources, rendering it virtually impossible for Gazans to feed themselves—now and in the future.

In 2020, Gaza's farmers exported produce worth around $16 million despite the Israeli blockade, and farmers produced enough vegetables, fruits, eggs, milk, meat, and fish to meet around a third of local demand. A quarter of the enclave was farmland, according to the most recent agricultural census. Many families had fruit and olive trees, which are a symbol of connection to the land and are passed down through generations.

Mohamed Ahmed is a Bedouin farmer from Al Salam, a village in southern Gaza near the Rafah crossing. Before the war, Mohamed, forty, had thirty sheep and olive and pomegranate orchards on land that he inherited from his father. He also worked as a history teacher at the local school and told me that his family had a comfortable house and a car. On May 6, 2024, Israeli forces went ahead with a long-threatened ground operation in Rafah, where more than a million displaced people had been told to shelter. "Israeli officials knew precisely the devastation the ground operation in Rafah would inflict on Palestinian civilians," said Amnesty International.

Mohamed was among 275,000 or so people with homes, land, and businesses in Rafah, who were forced out and unable to return. "I am now begging humanitarian organizations to give me food. All my trees were bulldozed. All my sheep are dead. My cousin's water well was blown up. The

UNRWA school was bombed. Everything was destroyed, and the military took over. Our land was paradise and became hell."

Mohamed was messaging me from the Mawasi IDP camp in Khan Younis, about twenty-five kilometers from Rafah. He shared a video of his cousin's well and water tank being blown up, the explosion unleashing a thick gray smoke that spread over the rubble of flattened homes, and orange and olive trees. Mohamed's land was 800 meters south of the well, which had supplied several villages in eastern Rafah. In the camp, the family received twelve liters of water each per day—more than some in Gaza, but still way short of what humans need to thrive. It had been months since the family had eaten fruit or meat, and his three children aged three to thirteen were cold and hungry, he said, as he sent me photos of sprouting onions and arugula that he'd planted outside the tent. "The land is a source of joy and pride for us. They want to displace us, but we would never abandon our land. We must remain strong in the face of hardship . . . this is *sumud* [steadfastness]. We love our homeland as much as we love our children."

According to a Forensic Architecture investigation, 104 square kilometers of agricultural land was destroyed between October 2023 and the end of June 2024. In other words, a staggering 70 percent of Gaza's fields and orchards filled with strawberries, tomatoes, sweet potato, wheat, eggplant, citrus, dates, and olives have been bombed and bulldozed. More than 3,700 greenhouses in Gaza, 45 percent of its total, were also destroyed. The beehives are gone. Almost 95 percent of the cattle, and more than half the sheep and goat herds are dead.

The destruction of agricultural lands and infrastructure was carried out using military equipment and weapons and repeated even after all Palestinians—including Hamas fighters—had been killed or forced to leave. It was not collateral damage or haphazard, it was deliberate and cumulative. After razing buildings and agricultural lands, the military has constructed roads, bases, and checkpoints, contaminating the soil and thus inhibiting future use, Forensic Architecture found.

"This is not just about killing people, it's about killing a Palestinian as a Palestinian. You disrupt their relationship with the land, the rhythm of everyday life, and their ability to imagine a future. You've changed the landscape forever. You've changed the flora and the fauna. It's now an alien landscape for people," said Michael Fakhri. "Gaza is not Gaza in ecological terms without the Palestinian people and their cultural practices."

Akram, the engineer, shared some photos taken in mid-2023 at his friend's strawberry farm in northern Gaza, which was one of the most fertile areas. It is now dusty, unproductive, cut off from the rest of the strip and under military control. "The north has been completely erased in what can only be described as ethnic cleansing. I doubt we will ever return to cultivate strawberries," Akram said. "I need to get my family out and start again, before they kill us. We have nothing here."

## Debris and climate impact

The Gaza Strip is just forty kilometers long and six to twelve kilometers wide. It has about the same land area as Las Vegas but with more than three times the people. The urban areas were tightly packed with apartment buildings, schools, shops, bakeries, universities, and mosques. By early September 2024, two-thirds of all structures had been damaged or destroyed, generating fourteen times more rubble than the combined total from all conflicts since 2008. The scale of the physical destruction is hard to comprehend, but nothing like this has been seen since World War II. UN agencies say it would take at least $50 billion and decades to rebuild Gaza— if and when the bombardment stops. Satellite images show that Israel has illegally expanded and further militarized several areas including the north and around Rafah—after razing every trace of Palestinian life. This means space to rebuild, if that happens, will be even smaller. New schools, homes, and workplaces will have to accommodate the huge number of amputees and other disabilities created by the war.

First the debris needs to be removed. Debris poses serious risks to human health and the environment, from the dust and contamination with carcinogenic asbestos, industrial and medical waste, heavy metals, and other dangerous chemicals from remnants of munitions including white phosphorus— which if used as an incendiary weapon in civilian areas is a war crime. The longer it sits there, the more dust filled with toxic particles will float into the air and seep into the soil and underground water sources. Also lurking under the rubble are thousands of unexploded munitions—which if handled inadequately could lead to even more serious injuries and amputations. So many solar panels have been destroyed, which will likely leak lead and other heavy metals into the soil and water, causing a new, long-term threat to the health of Palestinians.

It's hard to imagine what moving all that debris will entail, but one study found it could take trucks driving a total of *25 million kilometers* (15.5m miles) to transport 32 million tons of debris from the sites where buildings are destroyed or damaged. This is the equivalent of driving over 600 times the Earth's circumference.

"Our schools have always been bombed, our crops targeted, our villages destroyed, but the scale and intensity of the devastation of the physical and natural environment is unhinged. This is an unprecedented level of scorched earth," said the study's lead author, Samer Abdelnour, a Canadian Palestinian. "But what happens in Palestine doesn't stay in Palestine. This violence is going to have regional and global environmental effects."

The study also calculated the climate impact of moving the debris, estimating that the trucks would emit around 55,500 tons of carbon dioxide ($tCO_2$ equivalent/$tCO_2e$). This is on a par with the planet heating gases generated by charging 4.5 billion smart phones. Processing the debris with a fleet of 50 smaller crushers—the type primarily used after previous large-scale bombardments—could take almost thirty years and generate another 21,850 $tCO_2e$, the equivalent of charging 1.8 billion more smart phones.

It may seem callous to be concerned about the global climate crisis when the loss of life and immediate needs are so vast. But the State of Palestine is responsible for less than 0.001 percent of global greenhouse gas emissions yet now grapples with unprecedented climate events—in large part due to Israel's illegal occupation and warmongering. Globally, vulnerable countries which have historically contributed the least to global heating are being disproportionately hit by its impacts. Every ton of $CO_2$ now matters.

A separate study I first reported on for the *Guardian* found that greenhouse gas emissions generated by the first 120 days of aerial and ground attacks were greater than the annual carbon footprint of twenty-one of the world's most climate-vulnerable nations, including Tonga and the Cayman Islands. And more than 99 percent of the estimated 585,381 $tCO_2e$ (tons of carbon dioxide equivalent) emitted during the first 120 days could be attributed to Israel—the bombs, jets, and tanks, as well as the fossil fuels needed for generators and aid trucks in Gaza after the solar panels, water, and food sources were destroyed. Almost 30 percent of the emissions were attributed to the 244 American cargo planes known to have flown bombs, munitions, and other military supplies to Israel in the first four months. It's worth noting that a tanker of American military-grade jet fuel has been shipped to Israel every two months or so since the start of its aerial bombardment of Gaza but was excluded from the climate calculation.

But the biggest climate cost will come from rebuilding the schools, universities, hospitals, mosques, bakeries, and water and sewage plants deliberately damaged and destroyed by

Israel, which will generate an estimated 53.5 million $tCO_2e$. This is greater than the total $CO_2$ generated individually by 130 countries in 2023. It's a mind-blowing quantity of planet-warming gases to rebuild what Israel tore down, which doesn't even take into account the loss of carbon-absorbing orchards and other plant life that will increase the risk of desertification and further exacerbate the climate crisis. The Middle East is among the world's most vulnerable regions to climate impacts and the genocide in Gaza is exacerbating the global climate emergency—on top of the unprecedented death toll and human suffering.

"Even if you don't care about Palestine, even if you don't believe Palestinians have a right to exist, if you claim to care about the climate and the planet, then at least from a scientific perspective you should care about the emissions. Just look at the numbers," said Hadeel Ikhmais, who was unable to attend Cop29 due to a lack of funds.

Under current rules, neither the US nor Israel—nor any of the countries supplying weapons or oil to fuel the occupation, mass killings, and ecocide—will have to account for the greenhouse gases generated by military operations in Gaza or the other occupied territories. As David Boyd, a former UN special rapporteur for human rights and the environment, told me: "Armed conflict pushes humanity even closer to the precipice of climate catastrophe, and is an idiotic way to spend our shrinking carbon budget."

*Scorched Earth*

The destruction of Gaza and Gazans continued throughout 2024—in violation of the ICJ ruling in January ordering Israel to take all measures within its power to prevent genocidal acts. In July 2024, a separate ICJ ruling declared Israel's occupation of Gaza, the West Bank, and East Jerusalem unlawful, along with the associated settler regime and appropriation of Palestinian natural resources. And by the end of the year, multiple UN experts and international human rights groups had concluded that Israel was committing ecocide and genocide in Gaza—and that these actions must be understood as part of the decades-long strategy to erase Palestinians from their homeland.

The UN special committee to investigate Israeli practices concluded that its military tactics in Gaza are consistent with the characteristics of genocide, including the use of starvation as weapon of war and inflicting collective punishment on the Palestinian population. "By destroying vital water, sanitation, and food systems, and contaminating the environment, Israel has created a lethal mix of crises that will inflict severe harm on generations to come." In a separate report, Francesca Albanese, the UN special rapporteur on the occupied Palestinian territories, wrote: "Nearly a year of scorched-earth assault has led to the calculated destruction of Gaza . . . [this violence] is not happening in a vacuum, but is part of a long-term intentional, systematic, State-organized forced displacement and replacement of the Palestinians."

"This is a settler-colonial genocide, and the international court risks missing the forest for the trees if it doesn't consider the long trajectory that has led to the dispossession of the land, and the erasure of Palestinian identity and presence from that land since the very beginning," Albanese told me. "Israel's deliberate destruction of natural resources like the orchards and olive trees contributes to inflicting conditions of life made to destroy the group, and also the psychological suffering inflicted on the people . . . the land is who Palestinians are."

The Palestinian genocide is not the same as the genocide in Guatemala, but there are parallels.

"The Guatemalan scorched-earth policy was a way of driving people out forever by poisoning their homeland literally and spiritually, and creating such terror that they never return. Those who weren't killed were forced to stay in militarized hamlets," said Kate Doyle, senior analyst of US policy in Latin America at the National Security Archive (NSA). Then, the Guatemalan military rulers and civilian right wing were enraged by the UN policy of returning people in the 1990s— and the resilience of the Mayan communities who went back, said Doyle. Now, Israel's efforts to discredit, weaken, and eventually ban the UN agency for Palestinian refugees (UNRWA), is the culmination of a decades-long campaign to quash the issue of Palestinian refugees and their right to return. Neither the genocide in Guatemala nor in Gaza would have been possible without US financial and military backing.

"Instead of making the polarizing and incorrect analogy to Hitler's Germany, let's look at ways in which modern states have used scorched earth to destroy and drive out entire communities in the hope of destroying an entire people," Doyle told me.

In December 2024, an investigation by Amnesty International concluded that Israel had deliberately created conditions in Gaza that would lead to Palestinians' slow death. "The genocide doesn't stop when the bombs stop . . . displaced people are being intentionally sent to places where the military has already destroyed the agricultural land, the water sources, where there are no conditions to survive," said Erika Guevara Rosas, Amnesty's senior director for research, advocacy, policy, and campaigns. "This for us is fundamental proof of Israel's intention to destroy the population."

The environmental destruction orchestrated by Israel in Gaza and the occupied territories cannot be seen as an aside to the killings and forced displacement, but rather as a fundamental element in the ethnic cleansing and genocide being committed against the Palestinian people. Palestine is not just the place where Palestinians live, it is who they are as people.

# 10

# On Searching for Food in Gaza

## *Noor Alyacoubi*

It is quite absurd that a bag of flour has become my greatest comfort, a quiet reassurance that we might survive some more days. It doesn't matter if we find the flour infested with weevils; we'll sift it, separating the insects. That bag in the corner of our home is the only thing standing between us and the ghost of starvation. I no longer think of a grilled chicken or a dish of green salad; a loaf of bread is all that fills my mind.

From the outset of the war, food became our fiercest battle. When Israeli Defense Minister Yoav Gallant announced on October 7 the cutoff of essentials—food, water, electricity, and gas—I thought it was merely an intimidation tactic. I never imagined that I would end up yearning for bread.

I was naive to dismiss his words. But thankfully, my husband, Mohammed, saw things more clearly. Anticipating what was to come, he began to stockpile what he could: rice, macaroni, beans, and other essentials. He told me the war would last at least 100 days. I laughed it off, saying, "Impossible. You're exaggerating." We were both wrong.

When the war began, we had only one bag of flour, and we expected it to last no more than a month. Even then, flour was already hard to find. To stretch our rations, my husband, our young daughter, my brother-in-law's family of four, and my in-laws—eleven of us in total—decided to eat together. Like many in Gaza, we live in the same building, each in separate apartments. We believed that making one meal for everyone could save gas and make the food last longer. The first day of the war saw us emptying our freezers of any frozen supplies before they could spoil due to the electricity cutoff. That was the last time I remember having a lot to eat. After those early days, we started our strict regimen.

Each of us was allotted a small piece of bread for breakfast and a modest portion of rice or pasta for lunch. Sometimes, we would skip breakfast altogether to save our bread for lunch, but I always preferred to eat my portion in the morning, as breakfast gave me the energy to get through the day. As for lunch, I didn't care whether it was rice or macaroni. In all cases, it never filled me. Dinner, if we had it at all, was limited to a cup of coffee with a biscuit or sometimes just a banana, when natural snacks were still available.

Even in the best of times, I never felt full, but I also couldn't express hunger. My share was my share, and that was all. It wasn't a normal lifestyle to adjust to; it was pure survival. I used to satisfy myself with the occasional piece of chocolate to give my body a little boost of energy. And even the chocolate, my favorite dessert, failed to please my belly.

* * *

Soon, on October 13, things grew even worse. We woke up to the Israeli Army telling people to head to south Gaza, declaring it to be a safe area. We weren't sure of the news. But just in case, my husband and I prepared our emergency bags—if something happened suddenly, we would head south. We just believed what the Israeli Army said. We were idiots.

On the middle of the same day, I was standing before the window, looking at the sky and hearing the annoying sound of Israeli warplanes. Out of nowhere, I noticed a large number of papers falling all over the city. I rushed to the roof and caught one of the flyers. It said, "North Gaza is a war zone. You'd better head southward for your safety." I didn't react. I was just afraid. I asked my husband, "Will we go?" And he said, "Not yet. We don't yet know the reality of these flyers."

Less than an hour after the flyers fell, I found my father and older brother standing before my doorstep, their faces imprinted with fear and urgency. "Get your bags and let's go, Noor," my father appealed. I wasn't sure. Why was Israel pushing us to flee? Would the south really be any safer? I asked that we wait. "It's too early, baba. Let's see what's going to happen." Still, I was also scared for all of us. "Are you going to leave?" I asked. My father's kind voice ruptured the sound of violence raging around us. "I won't go without you, Noor," he said. He then got into his car and headed home, to the west of Gaza.

With every passing day, Israel intensified its efforts to force a mass evacuation from north to south Gaza, claiming it was for "safety." Bombs rained down on every street and building, specifically the western and northern parts of Gaza like Al-Karama, Al-Naser, and Al-Shifa neighborhoods, targeting anyone in their path in order to forcibly clear Gaza City of its citizens. We were caught between fleeing southward and holding on to hope. I found myself grappling with impossible questions: should we abandon our home and flee to the south with our precious daughter Lya, or stay and face whatever was to come? Would the south really be safer? In the end, we chose to stay, convinced that death would find us no matter where we went. On the other hand, my family stuck to their decision not to leave their home. But on November 2, just as Israeli tanks were meters away from their neighborhood, my family also decided to flee. Miraculously, under heavy shelling, they made it to Khan Younis in south Gaza.

We faced the constant battle of trying to decide what was better—whether to stay where we were or to flee south. We decided to cling to our homes and fight the expected challenges: death, fear, and even the scarcity of essentials, as securing a bag of flour was a serious matter. One day while Mohammed was walking on Al-Nafaq Street, a car filled with bags of flour passed Mohammed. He changed his direction and followed the car's driver. But once Mohammed reached the car, it was already empty. Mohammed pressured the driver to get him a bag of flour, and he finally took Mohammed to the storage and sold him one for 200 NIS (about $55US)—a price far beyond what we used to pay (40 NIS, or about $11). Meanwhile, Mohammed remembered that his uncle, who had fled his home for the south, had left behind a bag of flour. He called him and asked if he could get it. We had secured two bags of flour—we felt pure joy and expected them to sustain the eleven of us for at least two months.

The relief didn't last long. Many of Mohammed's relatives fled their homes in western Gaza to seek refuge in our home, located in the center and under heavy bombardment. The number of displaced people kept increasing until, one day in November, our home had become a refuge for over forty-five relatives, all sharing our meals. Every room in our three-apartment building was a makeshift shelter, housing five to fifteen people, including children. We shared what little we had. Though the rations were ours, we didn't put ourselves above anyone else. We ate together and endured hunger together. With so many mouths to feed, we had to reduce portions, giving priority to the children.

Breakfast dwindled to crumbs of bread for the children, while the adults made do with bitter coffee or, on rare occasions, a little milk. Lunch was the precious meal; everyone had a small share of macaroni, rice, or soup. When it was *foul*—a dish made of fava beans—everyone felt grateful because it was the only meal that could make us feel even remotely satisfied. Dinner was often non-existent, unless someone was lucky enough to find something to buy.

I can still hear the cries of children demanding bread from their mothers. It didn't matter if the bread was plain or filled with something—they just wanted a full sandwich, not a quarter or half. I can still see the sorrow in the mothers' eyes, knowing they were helpless to fill their children's bellies. Mothers used to hide some snacks for their children so they wouldn't sleep without eating something.

Enduring hunger alongside heavy, unbelievable sounds of explosions, some of the relatives sheltering in our house decided to prepare their bags and head south. Though we were heartbroken at the goodbyes, there was a small sense of relief, knowing that fewer mouths to feed would mean a little more food for those who stayed behind. Yet, famine was still famine.

Later in December, the Israeli Army announced plans to launch a military operation in the Al-Daraj neighborhood, where we live, forcing us to flee farther west. My family house, abandoned in November due to the Israeli invasion of the entire neighborhood because of its proximity to Al-Shifa Hospital, became our only possible destination.

Al-Shifa Hospital had been a primary target since the assault on Gaza. The entire neighborhood was thus deserted, with its infrastructure entirely devastated—no water networks, no electricity, and no communication or internet. When we fled our home in Al-Daraj, we took our rations, but water was difficult to carry. We didn't anticipate the complete absence of drinking water. For almost seven consecutive days, we couldn't find any safe drinking water— not even half a liter!

During this time, thankfully, I had two bottles of safe water that I had brought from home before we fled. Fearing my then eight-month-old daughter would contract a virus from unsafe water, I carefully rationed those two liters to sustain Lya for seven days—for her formula, for drinking, and for her cereal, alongside breastfeeding. Meanwhile, my husband, our relatives, and I drank completely unsafe, salty water. It didn't even wet our throats; we drank it just to quench our thirst—and I wish it could have done at least that.

Desalination plants were in the then-besieged Al-Daraj neighborhood. Other plants elsewhere were old and in need of maintenance. After almost a week, we barely managed to get one gallon of drinking water, unsure if we would get another gallon the next day. We had to divide the water again; everyone's share was half a liter. Our food was mainly cooked with salty water brought from wells—generated by some neighbors' solar panels.

By the end of January, we returned to our house in Al-Daraj, which had been greatly damaged as a result of the Israeli invasion and the bombing of our neighbor's home. Yet, we tried to wash the walls, to close windows with ripped curtains, to clean the whole house, and chose one good room to settle in. And this is the same thing all Gazans did after their homes were bombed or damaged.

Safe drinking water was available at times. However, white flour was already running out. The situation kept deteriorating until it reached its peak, when it was almost impossible to find even a kilogram of white flour anywhere else but in devastated homes whose owners fled to the south. People in north Gaza thus started to rush to their relatives' and friends' homes searching for a grain of flour, even if it was filled with weevils.

From the depths of despair, a reason to persist emerged and wheat flour surfaced. Though we weren't accustomed to it compared to white flour, its taste was acceptable. However, it soon disappeared from markets because of the huge demand. Out of nowhere, other alternatives also popped up, but they were mainly animal foods: corn and barley, smashed into soft flour. Their taste was beyond one's ability to bear it, but it wasn't a choice. It was a necessity. If we wanted to live, we had to eat it.

To lessen the bitterness of barley flour, specifically, we would sometimes mix it with grains of white flour—a portion of what little we did have. But soon the white flour completely ran out, leaving us fighting the terrible taste of pure barley and corn flour. For me, the corn flour is so much better than barley. I will never forget the day we tried to please our souls by making a pizza using a barley-flour pie. It tasted like hell, and I felt like an animal eating some grass.

We were forced to eat the green grass that grew by the sidewalks or in empty fields along with our animal flour: *khubaiza*. After months of fresh produce being absent in northern Gaza, the *khubaiza* emerged, though in old days, it used to be dismissed as mere weeds. It was something only our grandparents and ancestors used to forage, never bought for money. Yet then, its leaves became a lifeline, transforming into dishes that nourished us when nothing else could. We learned to cook it in various ways: Molokhiya, omelets, even pastries. It was the king of our everyday meal.

As the seasons shifted and the *khubaiza* waned, April brought unexpected relief. Markets overflowed with fresh vegetables and fruits, offering a respite from months of scarcity. Bakeries reopened, and the simple of joy of eating as much bread as we desired felt like a luxury beyond measure. And people couldn't hide their smiles anymore because of their happiness in carrying a bag of various kinds of vegetables and fruits for their children.

The crisis of the absence of flour ended, as Israel allowed the entrance of a good quantity of flour bags into the northern parts of the Gaza Strip. I thought the ghost of starvation that had been chasing us since October 2023 was gone, and we would be free. I cautiously thought I would no longer be hungry and I could eat as much bread as I wanted. The joy of eating some fresh produce, meat, and chicken did not last for too long, nor did it make up for the days we slept hungry or the food that had not been meant to be eaten by human beings.

Early in May, Israel announced the start of its military operation in the city of Rafah. Thereafter, the Karem Abu Salem crossing—the only commercial crossing through which goods and aid are allowed to enter the Strip—was forcibly closed, rendering the citizens of the Gaza Strip generally, and the north of Gaza specifically, to confront the specter of hunger once again.

Yet, starvation came in a new dress. White flour is here, but nothing else is. Yes, flour is valuable. I know how much it is worth. Yes, I lived days longing for even half a loaf of bread before sleeping. Yes, I dreamed of it.

We had managed to ration a good supply of canned food, as the war taught us never to trust good days, since the worst is always waiting for us. Since May, our only nutrition was canned foods, which was much worse than even I had expected. They taste very bad and are full of preservatives. The only difference between now and before is that before, I never felt full. Now, I feel full because I devour huge amounts of bread, though I know my body is eroding. I now long for a fresh green apple, a red, sexy tomato, and for a grilled fish with potato. My body is calling for healthy food. My body is worn out.

Six months before the war began, I welcomed my first child, Lya, into the world. She was my joy, filling my heart and days with the pleasures of motherhood. Every little detail about her fascinated me—her toys, her tiny clothes, her sleeping rhythms. I couldn't wait for her to experience life and taste all its flavors. I eagerly anticipated making her first meals, mashing fruits and boiling vegetables, watching her tiny face light up with new discoveries. But I held back on weaning, choosing to wait until she was ready for solids at six months. Breastfeeding was a beautiful, intimate bond, and I wanted her to have every benefit I could give.

After giving birth, I was meticulous about my own diet, eating only what would benefit Lya and avoiding anything that might cause her discomfort. Each morning before work, I'd pack a lunch box with a cucumber, an apple, a piece of cheese, a slice of whole-grain bread, and a bit of dark chocolate for energy. The long hours away from Lya didn't deter me from breastfeeding; I made sure to pump milk at work so she wouldn't miss out on the benefits of breastmilk. I was committed to giving her the best possible start, knowing that breastmilk was both the purest nutrition and the deepest bond I could share with her, even when I wasn't by her side.

Once the war began, however, our lives were upended. Survival took over, each decision tinged with scarcity. And amid it all, breastfeeding became my internal battleground. I was caught in a relentless cycle, exhausted and starving while feeling an unshakable guilt that I couldn't do more for my baby, Lya. Each day was an exercise in survival, each choice a struggle between necessity and scarcity.

She was growing day by day, with her need for food increasing. I forcibly reduced her share of milk from three times to two and her portions of cereal from three to one, although I rationed a decent supply of essentials for Lya. Days were passing by, and her needs were growing. On the other hand, rations were running out with no alternatives available in markets or pharmacies. I had no choice but to feed her whatever was around. Some days, that meant giving her bits of macaroni, or rice cooked in brackish, unsafe water. Every bite she took filled me with guilt, knowing these scraps were far from what a growing baby needed. I felt helpless, fearful of what these makeshift meals might do to her fragile body. I tried to believe I was doing my best, clinging to any small assurance that my efforts counted. But in those quiet hours of night, the guilt would rise, and I'd find myself questioning—was my best ever going to be enough?

I maintained breastfeeding, though I always felt inadequate as my own nutrition had dwindled to scraps, leaving me weaker by the day, my energy slipping away. My body was breaking down, thinning from seventy-three kilos to a fragile sixty, losing not only strength but the essential nutrients Lya needed from my milk. Each feeding left me more drained, but I pushed away the thought of weaning Lya. I was determined to give her every drop I could, even as it came at the cost of my own health. I used to tell myself that any small drop was still something—a piece of me I could give.

I kept fighting until I fell in pain. My breast tissue ached with each feeding due to the scarcity of breastmilk, and I knew, painfully, that I had to let go. The day I decided to wean Lya felt like defeat, a moment I had fought so hard to avoid. She was already a year old. I had no choice—I was simply too depleted. I weaned her, and my heart broke, as though a part of our bond was severed, leaving me feeling as if I had somehow failed her.

Amid the turmoil of what to feed Lya and what to make for her in the absence of any fresh, healthy nutrition, some kinds of vegetables started to pop up in street markets brought from farmers who managed to plant seeds in their gardens or lands, especially field pumpkin, which I used to make soup with some rice. The prices are exorbitant, but it's worth it if it means she can have something fresh. Lya is nineteen months old now, and there are still so many things she has yet to taste—a red tomato, a banana, a strawberry, yogurt. All these small pleasures that most children know are still mysteries to her.

Through every day of this struggle, I cling to the hope that someday, her world will be full of colors and flavors again. I dream of her tasting her first bite of something sweet, of her growing strong and healthy in a life beyond war and scarcity. But for now, we survive, and I hold on to the strength I have left—for her, for us, for the day when she'll finally know all the things I've been waiting to give her.

# 11

# From Cradle to Grave

*Dr. Tanya Haj-Hassan, as told to Fatima Bhutto*

When I arrived at Al-Aqsa Hospital in March 2024, I had certain expectations based on what I'd seen on social media and heard from colleagues who had been there before. But nothing truly prepares you for the sights, sounds, and smells.

There was a mass casualty incident that I remember vividly. I thought it was an isolated, horrific event, only to realize this was a regular occurrence. These incidents happened every few hours, often leaving barely enough time to mop up the blood, clear the resuscitation room, and start over.

There wasn't enough space in the hospital to admit all the patients. They were in the corridors, in front of elevators, on stairwells—places that would never have been clinical areas before October of last year. Every corner of the hospital was being used.

The volunteer physicians shared cramped sleeping quarters—one room for women and one for men, but even as volunteers we had more space and amenities than the patients or their families. I remember walking in wearing scrubs and a stethoscope. Family members would immediately rush to me, pleading, "Doctor, please help my son. Give him something for the pain." It was devastating to realize that many injured patients were in untreated pain.

The diversity of patients and the sheer scale of suffering was overwhelming. Mass casualties brought in dozens—sometimes hundreds—of patients. The cases were triaged based on severity. Green was for minor injuries, yellow for those needing urgent care, and red for patients requiring immediate resuscitation. I was based in the red area, which technically had room for three beds. We ended up placing patients on the floor, in the walkways, and even outside the red room. It was chaotic, and many who should have been classified as red couldn't even be accommodated there.

As a pediatric intensive care doctor, I primarily treated children. Normally in war zones, pediatricians are less busy because casualties reflect the battlefield: They are predominantly young men. But in Gaza, the demographic was "cradle to grave." We saw patients of all ages—infants, toddlers, children, adults, and the elderly. Children seemed to make up a large proportion of the injured. Entire families of children came in, often with parents telling us that others were still trapped under rubble. The injuries were mostly due to aerial bombardment. We saw primary blast injuries affecting internal organs, secondary injuries from shrapnel penetrating or slicing through, tetiary injuries from crush or displacement trauma, and quaternary injuries, such as severe burns—some with over 95 percent of their bodies burned.

Burns like that are usually a death sentence, particularly in Gaza, where resources are so limited. Tragically, these children often died slow, painful deaths because we didn't have the resources—human, space, medications, or materials—to provide them with dignified palliation. We also treated penetrating injuries, including gunshot wounds. I remember one child who had a gunshot wound to the head; it was fatal.

Beyond trauma, we saw children with preventable illnesses: hepatitis A and fulminant liver failure, severe pneumonia, and skin infections. These were consequences of destroyed water systems, sanitation, and the lack of basic supplies like soap. When you destroy sewage systems, water infrastructure, and shelters, and block essential items like soap or seeds from entering Gaza, epidemics of disease and malnutrition are inevitable. These actions seem intentionally designed to make civilian life unsustainable.

This aggression targets the entire population of Gaza. However, children are vulnerable in unique ways. Younger children can't run or evacuate as quickly, and older children might lag behind during family escapes. There are also documented cases of children being intentionally shot, sometimes in the same areas of the body, suggesting deliberate targeting. For instance, a friend of mine in Gaza shared the story of a ten-year-old girl shot in the chest while fleeing; another child was shot in the same spot two days later. Despite attempts to resuscitate them, no one was able to save them.

\* \* \*

Gaza is different than other conflict areas I've worked in in several ways.

Demographics: The violence indiscriminately targets civilians of all ages and genders.

Entrapment: Unlike in other war zones, Gazans cannot flee. There's no safe zone. So-called safe zones where civilians are forcibly transferred have repeatedly been targeted by the Israeli military.

Media blackout: International journalists and investigators are banned, making this genocide largely unseen by the world.

Aid restrictions: Gaza is blockaded by land, sea, and air. The very state responsible for the genocide controls humanitarian aid entry.

Targeting of aid workers: Rescue workers, healthcare providers, and journalists are being killed at unprecedented rates.

On top of this, healthcare facilities have been consistent targets. Since October of last year, every hospital in Gaza has been attacked in some way—through airstrikes, besiegement, or the denial of fuel and supplies. This is not new; it has been documented with many previous aggressions on the Gaza Strip, but this time it has been so systematic that it has annihilated the healthcare sector. Ambulances are also targeted, often in double and triple strikes, hitting rescue workers after the initial attack.

It's true that rebuilding what Israel has destroyed is possible if there's international will and political support. However, it would take decades just to clear the toxins, carcinogens, and teratogens from the bombings, let alone rebuild infra-structure. Gaza's healthcare system—and its society—has been deliberately decimated. Every person I met in Gaza has lost multiple loved ones and witnessed unimaginable horrors, and they have all lost their homes. Many children have lost their entire families. The trauma inflicted on this population is incomprehensible.

The world's silence in the face of this genocide is horrify-ing. My question is not just how Gaza will recover—but how the rest of the world, which allowed this to happen, will ever recover. I don't know if we can.

# 12

# A Home for Art in Gaza

*Shareef Sarhan, as told to Sonia Faleiro*

Art has always been a way for me to survive. In Gaza, where life is defined by borders, blockades, and bombings, creativity becomes not just an expression but a necessity. It was this belief that inspired me to create *Shababeek*—a space for artists to dream, experiment, and share their work with the world.

Shababeek began as an idea to open opportunities for both young and established artists. Every season, we announced an open call and selected six participants—three men and three women. Over the course of three months, we provided them with space to work, a stipend, and the logistical support they needed to create freely. Beyond that, we connected them with curators and artists from outside Gaza. These connections allowed them to expand their ideas and discuss new techniques and materials.

For university students, we introduced *Wasla*—a special program named after the Arabic word for "connection." Gaza's art colleges tend to focus on traditional disciplines like painting and art history, but modern forms like video art, performance, and critical art are largely absent. Through Wasla, we taught students how to develop concepts, write about their ideas, and practice new techniques. It was an effort to expose them to global perspectives while empowering them to reflect their own realities.

Before Shababeek, artists like me gathered wherever we could: in cafés, public spaces, and makeshift studios. Shababeek became a sanctuary—a home where we could showcase our work without interference.

Over time, Shababeek became one of the few spaces in Gaza dedicated to visual art. It was a hub for local and international audiences, a platform for artists to express their individuality, and a place to challenge the often one-dimensional narratives about Gaza. On opening days, our exhibitions attracted 200 to 250 visitors. For me, Shababeek was love and life—it gave Gaza a new face, a face of creativity and resilience. It was a symbol of hope in a place where hope is constantly under siege.

But Shababeek, like so much else in Gaza, could not escape the violence. The first attack came in December 2023 when Israeli airstrikes near Shifa Hospital damaged our solar panels. Solar power was essential for us because electricity in Gaza is intermittent at best. Then, in March 2024, the final attack came. The bombing destroyed the entire area, reducing Shababeek and everything inside it to rubble. My brother, who still lives in Gaza, confirmed the worst: nothing could be salvaged.

The loss is immense. Shababeek was more than a building—it was a vision of what Gaza could be. Even now, I cannot fully process its destruction.

For me, the grief is compounded by exile. I left Gaza in August 2023 to visit my family in Istanbul. It was meant to be a short visit; my children study there, and I wanted them to have opportunities beyond the confines of Gaza. I wanted them to experience a broader world, to dream bigger than our borders allow.

When the bombings came, I was far from home. A friend sent me the first picture of the destruction via Instagram. I immediately called my brother, who confirmed that Shababeek was gone.

In the months since the destruction of Shababeek, I have struggled to create. How can one make art in the shadow of genocide? Yet, I must. Art is how I support my family, how I pay for my children's education, and how I stay connected to the spirit of Gaza. I have joined artist residencies abroad, finding solace and support in temporary spaces where I can begin to rebuild my practice. Still, selling art is not easy. Each piece feels like a fragment of home—a home I may never return to.

Shababeek lives on—not in its physical form, but in the memories of those who passed through its doors, in the connections it fostered, and in the art it inspired.

# 13
# Final Earth
## *susan abulhawa*

As Israel laid Gaza to waste, a vast collection of terrifying explosions were broadcast around the world. Often in these videos, one could see the narrow escape of birds emerging from the plumes of smoke and debris, through and out of the frame. Few, if anyone, notice them. But like the humans in those videos, they had just lost everything— their nests, their kin, their refuge, and their sense of place in the world.

Given that Israel has destroyed 83 percent of all plant life in Gaza, their food sources are also gone. The bugs, the bees, the spiders, and seeds they rely on are no more, and with them go the rodents, geckos, porcupines, groundhogs, snakes, and all other flying, crawling, slithering, hopping, and scurrying life forms up the food chain.

*Where do birds fly after the last sky?*

Palestine is a vital resting hub where Africa, Asia, and Europe intersect for at least a billion migrating birds. The *Palestine*

*Corridor*, or the *Via Maris*, is the second busiest bird migration path in the world for thousands of species. Every autumn and spring, various locations throughout Palestine, including the Wadi Gaza wetlands, host millions of birds, who come to their ancient lands to replenish their strength after flying thousands of miles from their wintering grounds in Africa to their nesting and breeding places in Europe and Asia.

But Israel has obliterated the Wadi Gaza wetlands. Their unceasing airstrikes and artillery have devastated that sensitive ecosystem, disrupting and polluting the soil, water, and vegetation. We still do not know the true impact or long-term consequences for migrating birds and biodiversity in the region, but it is likely that Israel has driven hundreds of species into extinction. We can be sure, however, that tens of thousands of birds, along with all manner of vertebrate and invertebrate life, have been killed directly from Israeli fire, or indirectly from pollution, destruction of habitats and food sources, disturbances, and noise of military explosions that disorient sensitive creatures of the land, sea, and sky. It is estimated that approximately 250 species of birds will become extinct because of Israel's genocide in Gaza—all manner of waterfowl species, waders, and raptors, reptiles, and mammals.

This is not the first time Israel has ravaged ecosystems in Palestine in pursuit of colonial domination. While Zionists love to claim they "made the desert bloom"—one of their many branding slogans (Israel is the only country in the world that invests hundreds of millions of dollars in branding campaigns, like all charlatans peddling junk)—Israel, in fact, did the exact opposite in significant loci of biodiversity in Palestine.

For example, in the 1950s, at the time that they commissioned Leon Uris to write *Exodus*, their magnum opus of propaganda to market their colony to Western masses, Israel was draining the Hula wetlands, which they dubbed a "malaria swamp." The project was meant to showcase Zionist ingenuity and pioneering, whereby Jewish Europeans declared they were "healing the land," which they claimed had been left to fester by backward natives. In reality, these foreign settlers destroyed an enormously lush ecosystem, teeming with fish, birds, plants, and wildlife, some of which were exclusive to the region. It was a vast regional biodiversity treasure that had been a vital stop for migrating birds and millions of other life forms, all of which were decimated. Millions of birds died, and many species of life became extinct as a result.

Zionist colonizers drained those glorious ancient wetlands in order to build Jewish-only settlements in their place, all of which soon collapsed, as the land itself rejected them. Destroying an entire ecosystem led to significant erosion and underground fires that could not be extinguished, which were caused by heat generated from oxidation of dry peat and other materials that released nitrates as they burned, causing the soil to become infertile. Within a mere few years of this "Jewish ingenuity," the entire area became a giant wasteland. They had turned a regional treasure trove of life and biodiversity into a veritable desert of weeds and field mice. They literally turned bloom into desert.

In many ways, this episode in the chronicles of Israeli colonial crimes and stupidity serves as something of a metaphor for the entirety of the Zionist project. It was an ambitious enterprise to "heal," touted as genius, and conceived by foreigners ignorant of the local terrain, its history, and ecology, eager to solve, civilize and lay claim, sure of their own glory; but in reality, it was profoundly harmful, misguided, antithetical to life, and doomed to failure.

## Dogs of war

Thousands of miles away in the Netherlands and Germany, various dog training companies, most of which operate in secrecy, provide Israel with a continuous supply of Belgian Malinois Shepherd dogs, trained to attack on command and accompany soldiers in combat. Putting aside the ethics (which shouldn't be put aside) of breeding and training sentient and sensitive animals to be used as disposable weapons, Israel has used these highly intelligent and social dogs as purveyors of violence and oppression. There are dozens of documented instances of these dogs mauling Palestinians, including children, on command throughout the West Bank before October 2023. Since the Israeli military entered Gaza, they have used these dogs to scout tunnels and buildings for resistance fighters, often leading to the demise of these dogs.

There have also been many documented instances of Israeli Occupation Forces dog maulings in Gaza, one of the most heartbreaking was the story of Muhammad Bhar, a young man with Down Syndrome in Shujaiya. He had tucked himself into a corner when Israeli soldiers stormed into his home, unleashing their dogs and drawing their weapons on the family. The dogs immediately attacked Muhammad, mauling his face first and then latching onto his arm. Muhammad had been non-verbal all his life, and in that terrifying moment, as his besieged family pleaded with the soldiers to get the dogs away from their son, his mother and siblings heard Muhammad speak his first words. *Bas ya habibi, khalas.* "Stop my love, that's enough," he said to the dog, clearly repeating the tenderness he had heard all his life. He would not have understood what was happening to him— why his family had moved from one place to another; why so many explosions surrounded him; why those terrifying people were in his home; why these dogs hated him, what they were doing to him, or why his blood was gushing around him. As Muhammad screamed, soldiers expelled everyone from the home except him, and they moved him into another room. Alone, they left him to his fate. Seven agonizing days later, when the military withdrew, the family rushed to retrieve him, only to find his body decomposing, worms swirling in his face.

Israel has systematically used these dogs against unarmed civilians, including hospital patients and staff, the elderly, toddlers, and young children, as well as Palestinian captives in its detention centers. Perhaps for the first time in the history of terrorism, there are disturbing testimonies that Israel is using dogs to rape Palestinians.

## Dogs of resistance

It did not take long for Gaza's stray dog communities to figure out the cause of the terror suddenly blanketing their lives—the bombs, the booms, the blood, the death, the rubble. By February 2024, Israeli soldiers began reporting large packs of aggressive dogs attacking their military gatherings, snarling, and trying to bite them. The dogs knew, in that precious intuitive way of dogs, that these particular humans were the enemy. Palestinian media reported on the subject with such headlines as GAZA'S STRAY DOGS JOIN THE RESISTANCE. Israeli sources dismissed their behavior as a normal hunger response. There's no doubt that Gaza's animals, like her humans, were starving. In fact, there were reports and horrifying videos showing stray animals feeding on human corpses littering northern Gaza, where Israeli soldiers prevented relatives from retrieving their loved ones. But the hunger theory does not take into account the complex social structures of dogs, nor the fact that there have been no reports of such aggression toward Palestinians. It would not be the first time dogs exhibited such agency, fighting of their own accord alongside oppressed humans. El Negro Matapacos, a Chilean stray dog, became famous in the 2011 student protests, where he led packs of street dogs against police violence.

Like their wolf ancestors, stray dogs live in social units called packs, which typically consist of parents, offspring, and extended family of grandparents, siblings, aunts, uncles, and individuals dispersed from other packs. While packs are territorial and fight with other packs, their behavior is always predicated on the preservation and overall life experience of their collective. It is not uncommon for warring packs to unify, because they have a keen sense of group interdependence and understand they need each other to survive. It is therefore not unreasonable to believe that the sudden and seemingly coordinated dog attacks on military gatherings was the result of purposeful unity to defend themselves and territories against a clear common enemy.

## *Some animals are more equal than others*

Israel's response to Gaza's stray dogs during the holocaust of 2024 has been to shoot them dead, as ordered by their Nature and Parks ministry. Contrary to branding campaigns aimed at painting Israel as an animal-friendly country, culling stray animals by shooting (widely considered inhumane) has been common practice in Israel, an abuse which is generally ignored by international animal rights organizations. In contrast, when the Palestinian Authority adopted this method to curb the stray dog population in the West Bank, condemnation was swift.

Israel's animal protection record is actually abysmal, but you'd never know that from international animal rights organizations. People for the Ethical Treatment of Animals (PETA), widely considered the leading animal rights advocacy organization, is quick to issue scathing statements against animal abusers, including well-deserved criticism throughout the Arab world. But their approach to Israel has

been to largely ignore their rampant animal abuse and ecological devastation, heap praise on the Jewish state, and even
publish misrepresentations of facts in order to bolster Israel's
image.

There is ample evidence of widespread, intentional, and
ongoing murder and destruction of animals and vegetation
throughout Gaza by Israeli soldiers, including sniper and
tank fire directly on horses, donkeys, sheep, and goats, and
the systematic decimation of soil, water, and air systems
tantamount to ecocide. Ignoring these Israeli atrocities,
PETA sent a letter to UN Secretary-General António
Guterres calling on the UN to provide aid to starving animals
in Gaza. The letter spoke of "the war in Gaza," without once
referencing Israel, as if Gaza were bombing itself and the war
was a matter of unexplained combustion; and as if the supply
of aid were up to the UN, instead of Israel, which controls all
aid entry.

In 2018, PETA published a blog suggesting that Israel was
the "vegan capital of the world." The article was updated
multiple times in subsequent years, seemingly part of a new
*hasbara* (Israeli propaganda) campaign, dubbed by
Palestinians as vegan-washing, as similar headlines were
popping up throughout Western media, both before and after
PETA's claims.

In fact, in the year in which their statement was first
published, Israel was the third biggest consumer of meat per
capita in the world, after the United States and Australia. In
the following year and since then, Israel surpassed Australia,
becoming the second biggest consumer of meat per capita in

the world. Additionally, at 65 kilograms per capita per year, Israelis are the leading consumers of poultry in the world by a large margin.

Leading the world in consumption of animals hardly suggests "vegan," much less "vegan capital." Why, then, would a preeminent US-based animal rights organization deliberately mislead their supporters to peddle a foreign state's propaganda? I suppose one can ask the same question about Western media, which widely parroted unsubstantiated, sensational Israeli claims, all of which turned out to be lies, from forty beheaded babies to mass rapes on October 7.

The answers to these questions are beyond the scope of this article, but a phrase from George Orwell's *Animal Farm* comes to mind:

*All animals are equal, but some animals are more equal than others.*

## The saddest place everywhere

Mere days before Israel assassinated beloved professor, writer, and thinker Refaat Alareer, he and I exchanged messages about the Gaza Zoo, among other things. Israel had bombed parts of it and buildings all around it, sending the animals into a terror that made some of them psychotic, running endlessly in circles. Refaat had given a tour to local reporters, showing emaciated lions and monkeys, foxes that had lost their minds, and scattered dead animals. One zookeeper and his family took refuge in the zoo, doing their best to save the animals from starvation, and Israeli soldiers uploaded footage mocking a bewildered lion and what appears to be baboons that escaped the Gaza Zoo after Israel bombed it.

It wasn't the first time that Israel targeted the Gaza Zoo. During their 2008–9 bombing and invasion of Gaza, Israeli soldiers shot lions, monkeys, and other animals point-blank, even hunting down those that tried to hide in corners and clay pots. Those that were spared died of starvation, as Israel prevented anyone from feeding or watering the animals. Similarly, Israel bombed the zoo in 2014, killing most of the animals. The survivors had to be transferred to Jordan for psychological treatment from the trauma of deafening explosions. None have been evacuated during Israel's ongoing genocide in Gaza, which has lasted for fifteen months, as of December 2024.

In that last exchange with Refaat, we talked about rebuilding Gaza. We discussed schools, homes, and institutions. He agreed that there should not be another zoo in Gaza, that perhaps Palestinians could lead the way in ending this unethical and un-Islamic globalized institution that sees animals kidnapped, enslaved, caged, stressed, commodified, and forced to live unnatural, often traumatizing lives away from their homelands and kin, simply for human profit and entertainment.

Zoos in general, whether roadside or "state of the art," are probably the saddest places everywhere, made all the more tragic by the delight of children. Far from being spaces for education and conservation, a zoo is where children come to learn their first lessons in the supremacist ideology that gives rise to all other forms of xenophobia: speciesism. They teach children that animals are beneath us, on this earth for us to consume, experiment on, and toy with; to cage alone, behind bars, on concrete for our delight; to train through violence to dance and do tricks for our entertainment; to work for us; to die for us; to suffer for us. The animals in Gaza Zoo are first subject to the violence of captivity in cages so far from their homelands of lush prairies, forests, and savannas, and then subject to the violence of Israel's siege and bombings. Then they die by murder or starvation, anguished and terrorized. Refaat and I spoke of educating children when the "genocide is over." We were going to do this within the framework of their innate compassion and the tenets of Islam that prioritize freedom and mercy.

## The dignity of tortured lives

Because Israel has blocked fuel and gasoline deliveries into Gaza, donkeys and horses have become the primary mode of transportation. They are forced to work ceaselessly, ferrying people and supplies. Adding to their misery, there is widespread misinformation that donkeys do not feel pain as humans do, which means that cart drivers use whips and rods to make them move faster, causing festering wounds on their backs and rope burns on their legs and snouts, all of which are exacerbated by hunger and thirst, as Israel has also blocked food and water deliveries in Gaza. If these work animals are not killed or mortally wounded by Israeli bombing, they die of exhaustion. It is not uncommon to find their corpses among the vast rubble of Gaza, the sight of their bloated and decaying bodies adding to the apocalyptic landscape of what was once a bustling and resilient urban space of a high-functioning society, despite the siege and against all odds.

Like their humans, these animals deserve better. Donkeys and horses are gentle, humble creatures, who have borne the weight of history on their backs, their lives often marked by toil, neglect, abuse, and suffering at the hands of humanity. With their soft, soulful eyes, donkeys are creatures of remarkable resilience, carrying burdens beyond their capacity through merciless terrains, and in Gaza, enduring the terror of relentless bombing alongside their humans. In the Arabic language, calling someone a donkey is to label them stupid. Their torment is embedded even in language. But donkeys are sensitive and intelligent beings, capable of deep emotional connection despite the heavy demands placed upon them.

Though horses are held in higher regard as symbols of power and freedom, their lives are a far cry from either. Since the start of Israel's genocide, horses in Gaza are also used to move people and supplies around all day, having little to eat or drink. But even in societies that have plenty, these majestic creatures are relentlessly abused for entertainment and profit, from horse racing and the horror of "soring" to create an unnatural high-stepping walk, to nostalgic carriage rides in urban areas where they will live and die without ever feeling grass beneath their hooves.

Donkeys and horses are gentle creatures bound by a quiet grace that belies their mistreatment. Their willingness to serve is too often abused, but there is a way to see a profound dignity in their *sumud* despite the hardships and burdens they endure. Capable of affection, loyalty, and wisdom, they remain in bondaged service to human ambition through it all, but never entirely stripped of their inherent nobility.

## Culture of the future

Under the incessant buzzing of Israeli surveillance drones in Gaza, Saeed Al-Arr buys a tortured donkey from a cruel owner and throws his whip in the garbage, declaring "this donkey will never be hit again. He will never be forced to work another day. He will only eat and drink." Saeed, together with his family, run the Sulala Animal Rescue, an organization that has been feeding and providing care for stray and abused animals since 2006. They were forced to abandon their home and shelter where they provided care for over 400 dogs, 120 cats, and other animals, most of whom they were forced to leave behind. They opened all their dog food bags and left the gates open in the hope they could fend for themselves during what was thought to be no more than a few weeks of bombardment. On their social media was a heartbreaking video of hundreds of dogs running after their car from northern Gaza. The fate of those dogs remains unknown, with the exception of seven who miraculously managed to find their way to Saeed in the middle region of Gaza, months later.

In addition to cats, dogs, and a variety of small mammals

and birds, Sulala has focused their efforts on treating donkeys and horses during the ongoing genocide, establishing a free roadside clinic where cart drivers bring their work animals for treatment, and buying the most vulnerable among them to let them rest for the remainder of their time on earth.

Saeed Al-Arr's Sulala Rescue is not unique in Gaza. There are many groups and individuals working to feed and rescue animals impacted by Israel's genocide. Four days before Israel assassinated beloved Refaat Alareer, a video showed him feeding stray cats. He was already hungry at that point and had lost a considerable amount of weight.

The broadcasting of Gaza's annihilation has revealed so much about Palestinian society—the power and depth of their faith, their extraordinary endurance, defiance, resourcefulness, sacrifice, generosity, and the social bonds holding them steady. The world has witnessed their particular love of cats and their sacrifices to feed, rescue, and tend to animals despite their own trauma and scarce food and supplies.

As Israel decimates animals, leaving them dead, crippled, or traumatized, there are countless videos and reports documenting Palestinian individuals and Civil Defense rescuing animals from the rubble and doctors treating them; of Palestinians refusing to leave their pets even when they themselves flee from bombs or are pulled from the rubble bloodied and in shock; of them sharing what little food they have with strays; of them adopting strays and caring for them amid a genocide; and of pets comforting their displaced humans, or mourning them when they're murdered by Israel.

## The tenets of Islam

While cruelty and exploitation of animals is universal, Palestine being no exception, it is worthwhile to examine the teachings of Islam on the matter of animals, since Palestine and other West Asian and North African countries are Muslim-majority nations. Fundamentally, Islam regards animals as creatures of God, and its teachings emphasize the human responsibility to treat them with compassion, respect, and care, as well as providing clear guidance on merciful treatment for use in work or consumption.

The Quran and Hadith stress that animals have rights and should be treated with kindness and fairness. For example, Surat Al-Baqara (2:164) reflects the idea that animals, like all elements of creation, should be respected for the roles they play in creation. In Surat al-Kahf (18:9–27), which recounts the story of young men who sought refuge in a cave, Allah mentions their dog with tenderness and counts it as one of the companions themselves. Multiple Hadiths of the Prophet (PBUH), stress the oneness of creation and the requirement of compassion for the entry into heaven, as well as the punishment for harming animals. For example, he said, "Whoever is kind to the creatures of God, for he is thus kind to himself," and, "A woman was punished in Hell because of a cat that she had confined until it died. She did not give it to eat or drink nor did she free it." Also in the Hadith, a man's sins were forgiven by Allah for having given water to a thirsty dog, and a man was berated by the

Prophet (PBUH) to "give [his camel] its rights and treat it kindly."

The Prophet (PBUH) famously said, "Fear Allah in your treatment of animals." He forbade animal fighting and forbade making animals the objects of humiliation or entertainment, including caging of birds or other animals for reasons of amusement, which one can conclude means zoos as well.

Although Islam allows the consumption of animals for sustenance, there are strict rules undergirding its permissibility, what's called *halal*. The entire premise of a halal diet is predicated on compassion. Dietary halal rules establish conditions for how animals should be raised and slaughtered to ensure that the animal lives a natural life, free of cruelty or terror up to its final moment, when it should have no awareness of harm, fear, or pain.

Thus, when Saeed al-Arr trashes a donkey's whip and when thousands of desperate Palestinian refugees risk their lives to save animals or share their food with strays when they themselves are hungry, they are not the exceptions. They in fact exemplify the rules, teachings, and spirit of their faith. Theirs is the culture we need to forge a sustainable, equitable, and compassionate future that makes space for all of creation to thrive on this earth.

## Decolonization's central frontier

From the outset of Israel's genocide in Gaza, their leaders repeatedly referred to Palestinians in zoonic terms to justify their mistreatment and wanton slaughter. In fact, since Israel's inception, Zionists have labeled Palestinians as cockroaches, crocodiles, beasts, dogs, and snakes, among other things. Announcing Israel's plan for the starvation and isolation of Gaza, Defense Minister Yoav Gallant declared on October 8, 2023, "I have ordered a complete siege on the Gaza Strip. There will be no electricity, no food, no fuel, everything is closed. We are fighting human animals, and we are acting accordingly."

The tendency of colonizers to refer to native peoples in zoonic terms underscores what Alexandra Isfahani-Hammond has called "the entangled hostile structures of white supremacism and anthropogenic, or human-caused, violence . . . and drives home the shared fragility of non-white and animal life in colonial carceral reality."

Isfahani-Hammond laments the dearth of solidarity between mainstream animal advocates and decolonialists. She notes, "despite the interdependence of racism with speciesism, the anti-Zionist movement fails to center animal suffering while prominent animal rights platforms remain silent about Gaza," and indeed colonialism in general. A noteworthy exception, however, has been the climate justice youth movement led by Greta Thunberg, whose solidarity with Palestine has made her a target of smear campaigns from the same crowd that championed her before she revealed her moral consistency and their hypocrisy.

True decolonization requires a radical reimagining of power, justice, and sovereignty. Among the most overlooked victims of colonialism are the non-human animals, who have been subjected to exploitation, displacement, and annihilation within the same colonial systems that have subordinated Indigenous and colonized human populations. In this context, decolonization must be a multifaceted process that includes a solidarity with animal nations—an acknowledgment of their right to exist, thrive, and live free from the violence and domination imposed by human industries, agriculture, and ecological destruction.

Just as human peoples have distinct languages, territories, and ways of being, animals, too, exist in complex societies with their own forms of communication, social organization, and ecosystems that involve knowledge and cultural traditions passed through generations. These nations are collective communities whose existence is tied to their territories and ecosystems. Colonialism has eroded or outright destroyed these social networks, just as it has displaced human communities from their ancestral lands.

A sustainable future for humanity can only be achieved by rejecting the colonial mindset that sees non-human life as tools for or obstacles to human progress. Only a radical shift from domination to mutual respect and reciprocal care can carry us into a future that will care for all of humanity.

Ultimately, human liberation is predicated upon the recognition that our survival, dignity, and flourishing are inextricably linked to the well-being of the planet and all its inhabitants. Environmental justice, the rights of Indigenous peoples, and the rights of animals are not isolated struggles but interconnected threads of a larger tapestry of decolonization, because the capitalist, colonial, and industrial systems that oppress humans are the same systems that exploit animals.

It is in this spirit that we proclaim Palestine's rallying cry, *none of us are free until all of us are free.*

## 14
## On the Purposeful Killing of Storytellers and Truth Tellers

*Huda J. Fakhreddine*

*"Do you weep at every grave you see,*
*for a grave nestled among the sand dunes and low hills?"*

*"Grief stirs up grief," I replied,*
*"Leave me be! All the world is now my brother's grave."*

—Mutamim al-Yarbu'i, a pre-Islamic poet
who witnessed the rise of Islam, most famous
for his poetry in lament of his brother Malik

*I.*

On October 21, 2024, reporting live on the air, Anas al-Sharif's face goes blank. He looks down into a screen in his palm and reads: "A house belonging to the al-Sharif family, Abdulqader . . . twenty-two murdered in this massacre." He looks into the camera. You could see thoughts clouding his face, his eyes growing hollow, his mouth blank.

He had been reporting on massacre after massacre in northern Gaza for many months. The horrors have now fossilized into phrases that roll off his tongue. But this one didn't. It got stuck. He had to go back and start again.

> In the vicinity of Al-Qassam Mosque ... Of course, Abdulqader, one of the houses targeted belong to the al-Sharif family in Mashru' Biet Lahia. Of course . . . in this house was a large number of displaced people. Yes, displaced people. As we reported after yesterday's massacre, Abdulqader, the displaced sought refuge in relatives' houses. But now in this massacre, according to initial reports, twenty-two people killed.

He rearranged the information on his screen as if in the hope that a reordering of the phrases would change the reality. "One of the houses targeted belong to the al-Sharif family . . ." Did his mind wander in the neighborhood for a second, trying to locate that house, thinking to himself, do I know which one? Have I been inside? And then the many displaced people, twenty-two of them dead . . . was he going through a list on the screen or in his mind, going through names? Maybe the faces were coming to him, maybe specific moments. Of course . . . of course . . . it's a report and these are facts, and he stands there in his press gear, reporting it all, composed and steadfast, reciting everything twice, in disbelief, in horror, just to make sure, to confirm, to reject . . . "Yes, displaced people. As we reported after yesterday's massacre, Abdulqader, the displaced sought refuge in relatives' houses . . ." He adds information as if to buy time, to collect himself, information more general than the massacre at hand, information that would apply anywhere in Gaza, as if a deduction, a step back . . . "But now in this massacre, according to initial reports, twenty-two people have been killed."

"Are they your relatives?" his colleague's voice comes from outside the frame, as if from right next to me in the room across the ocean. "Are they your relatives?"

"Of course . . . of course, they are my relatives, Abdulqader."

What does the phrase "of course" even mean? Where is the "course" and where does it lead? In that moment when language was too scarce to contain what he was seeing, what his mind was feeding his heart, Anas leaned on the phrase "of course." He stood in front of the world, trying to make meaning, find sense. For Anas, the "course" had been one of sorrows, a path of pain. Was this his Golgotha, as an immense pain was inflicted on him, he unprepared, the world watching? How many Palestinians in Gaza have been put on the cross like this, on the cross of unfathomable grief, enduring the horror of their immeasurable agony, as a spectacle for a hardened world to see.

According to the Committee to Protect Journalists (CPJ) and other sources, Israel killed at least 130 journalists in Gaza between October 7, 2023, and November 2024, one of the deadliest times for journalists in recent history. Who knows how many more Palestinian journalists will be murdered for continuing to tell the truth? Israel kills before our very eyes, live on the air, deliberate targeting of the only voices telling Gaza's unspeakable story. On October 23, 2024, Israel announces a list of six journalists as targets, Anas among them. And yet, he continues to report. Standing among the dead corpses of his kin, his friends, his relatives. In hunger and in pain. In the cold and from the heart of the fire. He stays on the course.

Every journalist assassinated brings to the surface of our minds the murder of Shireen Abu Akleh on May 11, 2022. Shireen was killed by a shot to the head as she was reporting on an Israeli raid in Jenin. We will all forever remember her in her press jacket and her helmet, lying lifeless on the ground as her colleague Shatha Hanaysha tries to reach her, as her colleagues try to rescue her body from the monsters who do not even grant the dead respite. The shaky video that Majdi Banura, Shireen's colleague and cameraman, kept filming of his friend's death before his/our very eyes was supposed to bring the world to a halt. There it was! Caught on camera. A live shot of silencing, a reel of what oppression, injustice, and horror look like on a screen, undeniable, irrefutable. But like many recorded moments before it and many after it, it didn't.

On November 5, 2024, as the world was distracted by the farce of the US election, Anas was reporting on yet another massacre. He posted on X:

I always find myself wondering: What's the point of writing and reporting? For more than 400 days, we have been slaughtered from vein to vein. Has the massacre stopped? Has anything changed? Every day, we stand among the remains and blood, and what tears my heart the most are the remains of the children that haunt me even in my dreams. By God, the bitterness of betrayal is a thousand times more severe and harsher than the pain of aggression, war, massacres, displacement, and starvation.

But the world keeps turning obliviously, and we continue to be robbed of many familiar faces, trusted eyes and voices of Palestine. The cameraman Samer Abu Daqa, who was left to bleed to death on December 15, 2023, when Israel kept medical responders from getting to him. His colleague Wael Al-Dahdouh, *Al Jazeera*'s Gaza bureau chief, was injured in that attack. Hamza Dahdouh, Wael Al-Dahdouh's son, was killed on January 7, 2024, in Khan Younis. Wael was injured and his family targeted. Before Hamza's murder, he had lost his wife, Amna, daughter Sham, son Mahmoud, and grandson Adam. Ismail al-Ghoul and Rami al-Rifi were both assassinated on July 31, 2024, in an airstrike as they were reporting from the Shati camp near Gaza City. These are only a few of the *Al Jazeera* reporters who were targeted. The record of lives lost in the line of duty, on the front lines of our humanity as they told the story of those silenced, maimed, and buried under the rubble of international rule is endless.

Yes, of course, they are my relatives. Of course, they are me . . . and every corner of this world a grave.

## II.

*Ya waḥdana!* O How Alone We are!
                                        —Mahmoud Darwish, 1982

In 1982, the Palestinian Liberation Organization was exiled from Lebanon, and fighters and leadership were loaded on to ships and expelled into the sea. This was in the aftermath of the Israeli invasion of Lebanon and the horrific massacres of Sabra and Shatila, the two refugee camps where, as the records say, between 1,500 and 3,500 Palestinians and Lebanese where brutally massacred. And when the numbers falter, we know the actual sum of death is much greater than the hesitant numbers in brackets. Back then, the massacre was not live-streamed, but the photos of bodies piled up on the sides of the road—mothers, grandmothers, young men, children—are seared in our memory, indelible like a wound in the mind. And still nothing prepared us for Gaza, for the onslaught of horror after horror, the bottom of agony continuously moving out of reach, as day upon long day of genocide piled up.

In the aftermath of that horror, Mahmoud Darwish is remembered by his poets and friends to have said: *Ya waḥdana!* (O how alone we are!) A pronouncement of despair that wrangled grammar into submission. Darwish contorts the adverb "alone" into a noun and owns it with a possessive: our aloneness. He then steps back from it and addresses it with the quintessentially Arabic *ya . . . Ya waḥdana.* "O you, our alone-ness" is the impossible translation. How is it possible that we are this alone—left to our own bare, scarce devices—thwarted at every turn, massacred, sacrificed, denied, abandoned.

Variations of the phrase later made it into Darwish's resounding, agonizing, unapologetic lament, "In Praise of the Tall Shadow":

O how alone you were,
son of my mother
son of many fathers!
How alone you were . . .
The wheat is bitter in others' fields
the water salty and the clouds steel.
How alone you were!
Nothing can break us so don't drown entirely
in what's left of our blood.
. . . No roads, but you must walk
back, ahead, South, North.
You must measure your steps, balance them at the will of
    those who have granted you shackles,
[. . .]
those who decorate you and exhibit you
for visitors to see your glory
on display.
O how alone you were . . .
No need to write your final will, to say your goodbyes,
this is another exodus . . .

And Palestinians have been pronouncing their alone-ness to a hardened world for a long time. They pronounced it in

Dayr Yassin, in Tantura, in Kufr Qasim, in Jenin, in Tel al-Zaatar, in Sabra and Shatila, in Nahr al-Barid. In the First and the Second Intifada and the long wait for a third. In every assault Israel launches on the West Bank and Gaza Strip, before and after Oslo. During every expulsion of Palestinians from an Arab or non-Arab country. In massacres and confrontations, in peace and negotiations . . . Every day at borders, in airports, at checkpoints. They pronounce it every time they find themselves confronting a "progressive" or "reactionary" solidarity movement that reveals its hypocrisy at the first test.

On October 20, 2023, I heard it loud and clear. It echoed in my head and ricocheted off the walls around me. I was scrolling through the news on social media—still in what now feel like the early, distant days of the genocide—when Hiba Abu Nada's voice stopped me cold. A video of her pronouncing Palestinian alone-ness kept popping up because on that day the thirty-two-year-old poet who had a world of words and experience ahead of her was murdered in an Israeli airstrike on her family's home in Khan Younis.

> O! How alone we are!
> All the others have won their wars
> and you were left in your mud,
> barren.
> Darwish, don't you know?
> No poetry will return to the lonely
> what was lost, what was
> stolen.

How alone we are!
This is another age of ignorance. Cursed are those
who divided us in war and marched in your funeral
as one.
　　How alone we are!
This earth is an open market,
and your great countries have been auctioned away,
gone!
　　How alone we are!
This is an age of insolence,
and no one will stand by our side,
Never.
　　O! How alone we are!
Wipe away your poems, old and new,
and all these tears. And you, O Palestine,
pull yourself together.

Hiba's calm, unwavering voice addresses Darwish. "Don't
you know?" she asks him. "No poetry will return to the
lonely what was lost." Her resolute young voice addresses
her exhausted, battered Palestine. Embrace this alone-ness,
she urges, embrace this liberating despair and pull yourself
together.

Palestinian poets are destined to account for a Nakba,
remember a Nakba, and continue to predict Nakbas to come.
And every time we think that they have exaggerated or gone
overboard in their lament, their horror, and their despair of
the world, time becomes more unhinged and the occupier
more monstrous, proving the Palestinian prophecy true, time

and again. I believe Hiba's voice and I'm astounded by its immensity, its graciousness, and above all, its confidence. I want to believe its trust in a Palestine that is gathering in words, in streets and city squares around the world, a Palestine taking form every time a poem is read or translated, every time hope is resuscitated in hearts that insist on beating. I believe Hiba's voice and I want to believe its prophecy.

# 15

# Permissibility of Violence in Israeli Prisons

## Malaka Shwaikh

The subject of imprisonment has shaped both my academic work and my personal life. Several of my relatives have faced detention, including my father, whom Israeli authorities briefly imprisoned in the 1980s while he was a university student. At the time, arrests of students were widespread, and he was fortunate to be held for only a few hours. Other family members were less fortunate: My first cousin spent months in Israeli prisons, where he endured physical torture that permanently damaged his eyesight and overall health. Growing up, I was steeped in an enduring fear of imprisonment—even though I had committed no act that Israel officially deems illegal, other than simply existing.

Because family members and neighbors have been incarcerated in Israeli facilities, I have heard disturbing stories of the difficulties they face maintaining contact with loved ones—and of the profound suffering involved. This experience is shared by many Palestinian families, yet no level of anticipation can truly prepare one for the deprivation of liberty under a settler-colonial regime that operates with impunity.

Before October 2023, Israel held 5,192 Palestinians it classed as "security prisoners," a designation that Palestinians reject. They consider themselves "political prisoners" apprehended for resisting an illegal occupation. That number included approximately 1,319 administrative detainees held without trial or charge. Prisoners ranged in age from under ten to over seventy, men and women from all walks of life and political affiliations. Since October 7, thousands more Palestinians have been arrested and held for varying lengths of time, many ultimately released without charge. As of November 2024, Addameer Prisoner Support and Human Rights Association reported 270 child prisoners, 3,443 administrative detainees, and 94 female prisoners. However, no consistent Israeli statistics document how many Palestinians from Gaza are currently in Israeli prisons or detention camps. In an August 2024 report, B'Tselem noted that prisoners effectively "vanish off the face of the earth once taken into custody," a violation of Article 9(2) of the International Covenant on Civil and Political Rights, which stipulates that detainees must promptly be informed of the reason for their arrest and any charges against them. The practice also defies Article 9(1), which prohibits arbitrary detention and requires that liberty be restricted only on legally established grounds and procedures.

From 2016 to 2024, I conducted extensive interviews—both with former prisoners and with their relatives and solidarity groups—while researching prisons as arenas of power and resistance. In the course of this work, I uncovered substantial evidence of the use of physical, psychological, and emotional torture against Palestinians. Often, such evidence remains hidden. Israeli prisons are notoriously secretive; those outside the prison have little access and can rarely learn about conditions inside.

Because Palestinian lives remain a low priority for Israeli officials, the violence proceeds unrestrained. We see this in the collective punishment of the wider population: killings, starvation, the continuous bombing of infrastructure, and mass arrests. By labeling the Gaza genocide as a struggle between "light and darkness," as Prime Minister Benjamin Netanyahu did before the Knesset in October 2023, the Israeli leadership implies that Palestinians are considered merely urban *homines sacri*—lives deemed expendable. Within such logic, Palestinians become "bare life," existing outside state protection, their lives devoid of political worth.

*In Gaza—before custody*

> The quadcopter arrived at the hospital and started calling for those inside to leave. [Israeli soldiers started calling for us using the quadcopter]: "You will be safe." Once we left [the hospital], Israeli soldiers took us [into custody] and began hitting us repeatedly. We asked, "Didn't you say we would be safe?" They responded, "There is no safety." They continued beating us until we were transported to the prison. Settlers were hitting us, and it was normal. You'd tell the Israeli officers, "These are settlers," and

they'd reply, "He can spit on your face, too. It's not a
problem." (Witness, *Al Jazeera* interview, November 2024,
translated by the author.)

These words, from a young man in Gaza detained by
Israeli forces shortly after October 7, reveal how quadcopters
were used to order residents to evacuate hospitals and schools,
which had become de facto shelters. My own family in Gaza
recounts that these quadcopters can intrude upon everyday
life, enabling both targeted attacks and communication. With
them, Israel exerts dominance through persistent surveillance, regulating the conditions under which Palestinian
families either persist or perish. This tactic is not new: Gaza
has long been deemed an "open-air prison," an ongoing
strategy of population control that sanctions violent biopo-
litical measures and normalizes assault.

In addition to quadcopters, a September 2024 Human
Rights Watch report notes that Israel employs facial recognition technology to facilitate mass arrests—bolstered by an
extensive database of Palestinians compiled over the years.
Anyone deemed suspicious faces beating and indefinite disappearance. Prior to October 7, detainees would be taken from
their homes to prisons, where they might shuttle among
interrogation sites, courts, solitary confinement cells, and
other prison facilities, in no particular order. Since October 7,
the process has been even murkier: Prisoners are forcibly
moved to traditional jails or new facilities converted for that
purpose, creating an archipelago of "torture camps," as many
Palestinians refer to them. Over a dozen Israeli prison

complexes, spanning both military and civilian facilities, have been repurposed into spaces where torture is reportedly normal practice. Prisoners are crammed into increasingly overcrowded conditions, with many lacking such essentials as mattresses.

The mass arrests that followed October 7 have generated widely circulated images and videos of Palestinian detainees on social media, shared by both Palestinian civilians and Israeli soldiers. Scenes of torture inflicted on men of various ages—often blindfolded, handcuffed, stripped, and bearing marks of abuse—have found their way into mainstream coverage and social media posts. In November 2024, a correspondent for Israel's Channel 14 posted a photograph showing Palestinians stripped and blindfolded in Jabalia, northern Gaza; multiple witnesses report that many of those arrested were patients and medical staff from Kamal Adwan Hospital. Similar images have appeared in the BBC (December 2023), CNN (December 2023, October 2024), and Sky News (October 2024). In one photo, a man leans on crutches, while another still sports surgical drains from a laparotomy. Some have had limbs amputated due to excessively tight handcuffs or have been forced to wear diapers.

These visual records and testimonies point to major ethical concerns, including the apparent disregard of medical personnel's safety, and raise questions about the global community's limited response. If such treatment continues unchallenged, it risks normalizing violations of human rights in an environment with little accountability.

*Out of Gaza—after being taken into custody*

> I lost consciousness twice in front of [Israeli officers].
> While I was unconscious, they kept hitting me. [One
> officer] woke me up by torturing me, can you imagine?
> (Witness, *Al Jazeera* interview, translated by the author)
>     There was another guy, on the bed next to me—may
> God bless his soul. [The man cries.] He died before our
> very eyes [from torture]. A twenty-seven-year-old with
> blue eyes. (Witness, *Al Jazeera* interview, translated by the
> author.)

The experiences of these two men from Gaza underscore
the alleged indifference of Israeli officers to serious medical
emergencies, suggesting that torture has, in some cases, led to
the deaths of prisoners held in official facilities or temporary
detention sites. Once people are taken into custody, the prison
system becomes a highly clandestine environment. Except
for the accounts of those who are ultimately released, there is
scant visual proof of torture methods. Media outlets and
human rights organizations have documented prolonged
shackling of detainees—particularly those from Gaza.
Nevertheless, Israeli authorities often claim that no real issue
exists. A BBC investigation, for example, revealed that some
prisoners in Israeli hospitals were blindfolded, restrained to
their beds, and occasionally stripped.

Not surprisingly, reports of prisoners dying in Israeli
custody have spiked. By May 2024, the Israeli newspaper
*Haaretz* put the death toll from Gazan prisoners at

twenty-seven. B'Tselem, in August 2024, raised that figure to at least sixty Palestinians, forty-eight of whom were from Gaza—some of them dying before even reaching prison, owing to severe beatings en route. Sadly, this does not surprise me. The violence and isolation inside Israeli prisons create conditions in which settlers can commit lethal acts away from public scrutiny.

[Israeli soldiers told us], "We can kill you and leave your corpses behind." They ordered us to approach a check-point near the Indonesian Hospital. We obeyed. We were all civilians—children, women, the elderly, the sick. Suddenly, the army began separating out the men, elderly people, sick individuals, even children. In prison, I saw children under sixteen (they don't even have ID cards). I witnessed a young man, Muaz Rayyan, [dying from torture]. Another man [name removed by the speaker] was raped [by Israeli soldiers]. We need to get the voices of the Palestinian prisoners out. They're dying by the minute. Horrible torture. They take batons and insert them into prisoners' rectums. It's crazy. I left that prison with a mission: to relay the voices of those still inside. They pleaded with me, they were crying. They want their families to know about them. (Gaza witness, *Al Jazeera* interview, translated by the author.)

This middle-aged Palestinian man describes a harrowing ordeal. Families in Gaza are usually unable to ascertain the location or condition of their detained relatives. Family visits remain off-limits. This leaves families in a state of perpetual fear and uncertainty, an experience I understand personally. Even though I was never politically active, the possibility of a violent interrogation—and my own unpredictable responses—has repeatedly frightened me. I recall turning down a scholarship to study in the United States in 2012 because I knew that crossing the Erez border in northern Gaza would be a humiliating, potentially perilous experience, despite the absence of any wrongdoing on my part.

Israel's use of sophisticated technology—quadcopters and AI facial recognition software—further tightens its hold over Palestinian lives. Although October 7 represents a stark new chapter, it also reveals Israel's continued confidence that it will not be held accountable. As someone who survived Israeli assaults on Gaza in 2008 and 2012, I can attest that the psychological reverberations of violence are not limited to the present. Even after leaving Gaza, the faintest sound of a door slamming or the whirr of a passing plane catapults me to the past. The mental scars remain, inscribing a fear that endures long after the bombs have ceased to fall.

## The permissibility of violence

Despite everything, the former prisoners I interviewed frequently expressed hope. I recall a little-known 2019 documentary on Israeli prisons in which the reporter asks a Palestinian prisoner how one resists from within a cell. He replies, smiling, "By smiling . . . and by imagining victory. We will win in the end." This reflection suggests that hope is more than a vague longing for justice or freedom: It's a certitude, at least for some, that liberation is inevitable. But continuing to resist doesn't mean showing relentless strength or positivity. The expectation that Palestinians must always be resilient is dehumanizing. Narratives of perpetual resilience can gloss over the brutality of colonial oppression and reduce the complexity of the violence that Palestinians endure.

Hope, however, does have a role, especially for Palestinian prisoners who face escalating settler-colonial violence. Sustained by global and local solidarity, media advocacy, legal assistance, and constant reminders that they are entitled to political prisoner status, they strive toward justice and freedom. Yet hope alone, absent political engagement, is not enough to confront the unremitting assault on Palestinian existence.

# 16

## On Losing My Family—and My Mind

### *Ahmed Alnaouq*

On October 22, 2023, my family was sleeping peacefully at dawn when Israel dropped a bomb on our home, killing most of my immediate relatives in an instant. In the span of a single minute, twenty-one family members died, including my father, Nasri—a gentle, kind-hearted seventy-five-year-old man who could barely walk, weakened by illness and grief. Israel had killed my mother earlier by denying her the permit she needed to receive treatment for cancer, and they had taken my brother from us a decade ago.

Among those lost was my eldest brother, Mohammed, along with his two children, Baker and Basema, as well as my younger brother, Mahmoud, a shy twenty-five-year-old who had worked tirelessly to follow in my footsteps. He'd earned a scholarship to pursue a master's degree in international relations in Australia and was just months away from leaving. My three sisters also died, as did all their children—fourteen in total, all under thirteen. Some of these children were like my own; I had helped raise them, feeding them, changing their diapers, and taking them out when they were bored.

They were our joy and our future, slaughtered for a crime that neither they nor their parents had committed.

After the massacre, I called one of my brothers-in-law. He said he couldn't recognize his children: Their faces were unrecognizable, their heads crushed. I also learned that my older sister Walaa's body had been severed, with her upper half found tens of meters away in a neighbor's house. In my desperation, I begged neighbors to send me photographs of the remains, but they refused, warning me that I wouldn't be able to bear the sight.

In one minute, everything and everyone I cared about became a part of the past. My home, the place where I was born and raised, was now a heap of rubble and ash. No rationale can justify what happened. I've told this story every day since the carnage. And yet, I've insisted to friends that I've felt almost lucky—I'm alive, relatively safe in London, and not starving the way so many Palestinians in Gaza are. For months, that sense of being spared left me thinking of myself as privileged, even as I grieved. I still had breath in my lungs, whereas thousands of Palestinians who lost all their family remain under relentless bombardment.

That feeling of privilege followed me until last month, when I visited my friend Ahmed in Leeds. I'd been invited to speak at a film festival on journalism and the lives of Gaza reporters, and I went to see him immediately after. It was my first time seeing Ahmed in years. At least, I think it was—I suffer from memory lapses and have trouble concentrating. My last visit to Ahmed's new place, as far as I recall, was four years ago, back when I was completing my master's at Leeds University.

During the COVID lockdown, I shared a small, rented flat with two of my closest friends and fellow Chevening Scholars, Maisara and Bahzad. Both were doctors, immensely kind and brimming with talent and humor. They made that year—on top of all its uncertainties—feel almost normal.

At Ahmed's house, we revisited those days and, for the first time, spoke openly about losing our loved ones. We reminisced about Maisara, whom Israel killed last year, wiping out his entire family. Only his sister survived, because she lives in Austria—like me, she was far from the destruction. Until that evening with Ahmed, I had refused to speak about my emotions. Whenever the subject came up, I told myself that my feelings didn't matter. After all, I survived.

But that night, I confessed how I truly felt—angry, hollow, purposeless, and on edge. Most unsettlingly, I admitted that I'd begun to feel little empathy, as if numbness had stolen all sense of joy or accomplishment. Life and death had become indistinguishable. I also told Ahmed how guilty I felt for talking about these emotions when so many others have it worse, and I recounted my shame in feeling so "privileged."

Ahmed reminded me of the day Maisara was killed. Ahmed had called me, in shock, his voice quivering. He was weeping, furious, reeling at the news. But I had seemed oddly unaffected. I recall simply responding, "Yes, Maisara is gone," as though it were a banal update rather than the violent murder of our friend. Ahmed had been alarmed by my apathy, urging me to seek help before it led me somewhere dangerous.

On the train back to London, I had time to think. I remembered an incident from October 7, 2024, when I arrived home to find my wife in tears, staring at her phone. She was looking at pictures of her brother, killed by Israel the year before, his home bombed while he slept. "Stop crying," I told her. "You only lost one family member." She looked at me through her tears and said, "He was my brother, and I loved him." That simple statement cut through the callousness I'd adopted. It also reminded me of how my brother-in-law, Mustafa, had reacted after losing his father. He confided months later that he'd stifled his grief in my presence because he knew I'd lost so many more.

Yet over the last fourteen months, I've found myself increasingly numb. I see horrifying images: dead babies, people crushed beneath tanks, children sobbing at their parents' funerals. None of it brings tears. Paradoxically, a fictional film can reduce me to uncontrollable sobs. Real violence seems so overwhelming that I've become unable to process it; I lack the mental wherewithal to cry.

And so I ask myself: Am I truly privileged to be alive? Or is this half-life, laden with nightmares and insomnia, hardly living at all? Since the genocide began, I've traveled widely—across Europe, to Lebanon, Qatar, Malaysia—speaking at conferences and giving interviews. More people follow me on social media; I'm recognized at events. The life I once dreamed of—a life of travel, storytelling, and expanding my reach—feels hollow now. Nothing stirs in me but emptiness.

A few months ago, I was in Qatar for an education conference hosted by Her Highness Sheikha Moza. Staying in a five-star hotel, I gazed out from the top floor at Doha's glittering skyline. But instead of marveling at the city, I stood there for an hour pondering how shallow it all felt—money, luxury, opportunity. I used to crave these experiences, but in the wake of such loss, they mean little.

For fourteen months, I've resided in this vacuum of negativity. I sleep poorly—twelve hours, but mostly during daylight. I wrestle with nightmares every night, visions in which Israel is coming for me in Gaza. In these dreams, I'm shot, bombed, detained, or dismembered. The reality of new horrors in Gaza only compounds the despair.

Still, I hesitate to call myself unlucky. I think of everyone back home who endures these terrors in real time, bombed and starved, living every moment in mortal fear. If my own life feels too overwhelming to make sense of, how do they survive? And what will become of them, even if the bombs stop tomorrow?

This is the side of war rarely discussed, even by journalists and academics. Yes, genocide destroys cities and claims lives, but it also remakes the psyches of those it spares. It ravages entire communities and corrodes any sense of what it means to exist. The aftermath is incalculable, an endless echo that leaves no one untouched.

# 17

# The Bombing of South Lebanon

*Lina Mounzer*

What I remember most about that first day, October 8, 2023, is the heat—oppressive, unreasonably hot and humid, even for Beirut. The sun was obscured by what felt like steam. It was hard to draw a full breath—not just because of the heat, but from the apprehension. Between bouts of scrolling the news, I paced the house. By the first full day of bombardment, it was already impossible to comprehend the savagery of the vengeance against Gaza. And now, from South Lebanon, Hezbollah had declared itself a "support front." Restless, unable to stay home, my then-husband T and I decided to get out, to find somewhere else to be. The streets were eerily empty, even for a Sunday. The first café we tried was shuttered. So was the second, and the third. Everyone in the country was bracing for war.

We waited all day—for the war to reach us, for fire to rain down on Beirut from above, as it was on Gaza. But it did not spread, not that day, nor the next, nor the one after. Thus began a year of waiting: watching and waiting—through that first sweltering autumn, then the thunderous winter, then the beautiful spring and, finally, the hot summer. Watching the carnage in Gaza and waiting for our turn. But when the war finally came, I would not be there to witness the poisonous catharsis of its arrival.

All my life, I've lived beneath the ever-looming threat of Israel's wars. I was born the year of the so-called First Lebanon Invasion, when Israeli forces reached the Litani River. I was not yet four when they fully occupied southern Lebanon, then surged north, besieging and shelling West Beirut in an assault so unrelentingly vicious it made Ronald Reagan recoil.

I was about to turn fifteen when the Seven-Day War broke out; a fresh high school graduate when they perpetrated the Qana massacre—the first Qana massacre, for there would be a second ten years later—as part of their bombastically named Operation Grapes of Wrath. The first Qana massacre: One hundred people murdered when the UNIFIL compound—UNIFIL, the United Nations Interim Force in Lebanon, a peacekeeping mission tasked with maintaining peace and security in southern Lebanon— was directly shelled. That was back when people still naively believed that some places were safe from Israeli aggression. And between all that, over the decades, constant incursions into Lebanese airspace, regular strikes on bridges, roads, power plants, and an already ailing electricity network, and, often, just the simple sadism of low flyovers with their fighter jets, the supersonic booms so violent they sometimes broke glass, so loud we mistook them for actual airstrikes.

But before all that, and throughout it all, we were also always living with the result of Israel's foundational horror, its original sin: the thousands of Palestinians displaced from Northern Palestine into Lebanon in 1948, many of them fleeing the horrors of the Nakba on foot. Thousands were herded into refugee camps across the country; thousands more were integrated into every stratum of society. They were our teachers, doctors, grocers, bookkeepers, classmates, cousins, neighbors. And in their homes, their conversations, their accents, their expressions, and their regional varieties of Levantine cuisine, there were traces everywhere of the homeland they had been forced to leave. Our family friends kept the keys to their homes and the deeds to their land displayed prominently in their living rooms, and I grew up feeling the same pang of regret at the things they'd left behind—thinking it would only be for a couple of weeks—such as a prized gardenia plant left unwatered and a pot of stew uneaten in the fridge.

The Nakba was everywhere in the Arab world, impossible not to mourn: We lived among people undone by that loss, in countries entirely reshaped by it. This is why it's always seemed impossible to remain "neutral." We can't be, because we simply—geographically, demographically—aren't. The price of both resisting and submitting to Israel has always been violence. The choice is solely about whether to turn it inward or outward.

After 1967, when the Arab armies fell apart and it became clear that the Palestinians stood mostly on their own, the countries of the region were faced with a Faustian bargain.

"Help us suppress the Palestinians," they were told, "become our subcontractors in their dispossession and humiliation, and you will have (relative) peace." Thus, Israel never met an Arab dictator or autocratic regime it didn't embrace, and there wasn't a single Arab dictator who wasn't somehow grateful for Israel—for its convenient role as a valve to defuse popular anger before it turned on them. But Lebanon, with all its squabbling plurality, was impossible to unite under a single leader, leaving it, for better and worse, a place that remained permeable and open. By the time Israel, at the cost of immense bloodshed, managed to oust the Palestine Liberation Organization from Lebanon in 1982—since Lebanon, unlike Jordan, wouldn't, or rather, despite the best efforts of some factions, couldn't, do them that favor—we had our own lands to wrest back, and our own resistance groups to do it.

How does one live while waiting for a war of extermination to spread? One lives as one always does, except war is in everything and everywhere—following you into the shower, waiting at the bottom of your coffee cup, getting into bed with you at night, oozing its smoke into your dreams. Against every personal memory over the course of that year there is the war, the ever-present threat and fear of war. I remember the "milestones" of the Gaza extermination project better than I do the milestones of my life over the course of that initial year, especially those that seemed to portend wider war in Lebanon.

October 17, the night of the Ahli Hospital bombing, "the first hospital bombing," my friend J and I went out to dinner together for the first time since the war had begun. We hadn't seen one another since late summer, and then we'd all been shut up at home, watching the news, stunned and fearful. We are going to go to dinner and put away our phones, we promised one another. We are going to stay in the here and now, if only for a couple of hours.

But I couldn't resist. When she got up to go to the bathroom at one point during the meal, I picked up my phone. I saw the carnage. People incinerated as they sheltered in a hospital courtyard. It was still fresh enough that the Israeli tweets gloating about "killing Hamas terrorists" in a hospital still hadn't been taken down in a panicked attempt at covering up the crime and blaming it instead on a misfired rocket from the other side. This alibi would be taken at face value and repeated obediently by all the journalist-stenographers at all the major news outlets of the world. But we still didn't know that then. A hospital. We couldn't believe it. Surely this was the red line past which nothing could continue. Our meals grew cold as we scrolled and cried at the restaurant table.

Driving home, we found the streets aflame with the same rage that boiled in our blood. Burning tires at the major intersections; young men on motorbikes careened about with wild purpose. We heard they were headed to the American embassy in the foothills north of Beirut, taking their anger to the place where it belonged. Good. We heard there were midnight protests in Jordan. Good. Surely everyone would rise up against this abomination; surely the ferocity of the outrage would spark an inferno to burn the entire rotten world order to the ground.

But it fizzled, like the rocket they insisted had fallen short of its target. Soon enough hospitals were being assaulted—bombed, ordered to evacuate, set on fire, invaded—with such regularity that even soldiers storming in, kidnapping doctors and patients at machine-gun point, elicited no reaction—neither in the Arab world nor, certainly, abroad.

In mid-December, the Israelis directly shelled a group of Lebanese journalists wearing press vests and reporting from the border area. Reuters photographer Issam Abdallah, whom I'd never met but who was friends with so many people I knew, was killed instantly. Several others were severely injured. One of them, Christina Assi from Agence France-Presse, ended up at the American University Medical Center, and word spread across social media that she urgently needed blood donations. Having the right blood type, I went down to the hospital, where I found a crowd of about twenty-five to thirty people already waiting ahead of me, so desperate were people to do something, anything. The small waiting room was so packed that one girl, emerging woozily from the donation booth and finding no place to sit, fainted. Her sister, seeing her collapse, fainted too. More than anything, I remember the thudding fall of their bodies, the panicked commotion that broke out, and the medics who rushed to their side, shouting at everyone to give them space. A bloodless reenactment of a scene unfolding in Gaza hourly amid the smoke and fire.

We all made plans with one another for the upcoming weeks, always with the joking caveat, "war permitting." We felt guilty about celebrating festive occasions; we felt guilty when we didn't celebrate, given that we could. Restless and despondent, I went on long, rambling walks, heading down the hill from my house toward the sea, rounding the coastline from the ruins of the Holiday Inn to the Raouche Rocks, then cutting back in. Trying to memorize every detail of my beloved city before it was pulverized. I felt dangerously fragile, entirely permeable, as though there was barely any skin between myself and the outside world. I watched the people on the Corniche—the pot-bellied men speed-walking in pairs, the teenage girls passing their phones back and forth, giggling together on the benches, the parents and grandparents herding gaggles of shouting, tripping children, the young men exposing their gleaming chests to the sun and leaping off the rocks into the cold sea—and sometimes felt flayed open by an awestruck, painful love. This sweetness, this ease, this togetherness—all of it under threat. When it was the only thing anyone in Gaza, anyone anywhere, was ever fighting for: the luxury, the dignity of unhurried time.

At night, I lay in bed in our twelfth-floor apartment, exposed on all sides, the weight of the night sky oppressive above me. My body remembered the nauseating vertigo of how the building swayed during the August 4 port explosion in 2020, how it swayed during the February 2023 Turkey-Syria earthquake. My body anticipated how it would sway when shaken by the bunker-buster bombs surely on their way. If not that night, then the next, or the next week, or the next month. I forced myself to listen carefully to the silence, to appreciate its totality, though it made me feel entombed. During the day, I was able to function as usual, but night was when the terror came.

Some nights, when it seemed the war was very close, I made sure to have clothes and shoes beside me to pull on quickly if need be. Often it was impossible to sleep—or rather, to stay asleep until the sun came up. I would call friends in North America, awake because it was seven hours earlier there; I needed to hear a voice in all that darkness. They, too, were anticipating war; they, too, watching the carnage, felt diminished by it, waiting for it to spread to us. They went to protests and sit-ins and organized.

In Lebanon there was nothing to protest, nothing to shake a fist and shout at. We were a captive audience. Like prisoners held in a cell, listening to the torturous screams of the detainee next door as he is being beaten half to death, waiting for the guard to turn his attention to you. Gaza was—is—close. Just some few hundred kilometers down the coast. Same geography, same vegetation, same sea. When it grew unbearably cold in Beirut, we knew it had grown intolerably cold in Gaza. When it rained and thundered, we knew it was the same torrential rain falling on the ruins and tents of Gaza, the same thunder that people couldn't tell from airstrikes. It was so easy to picture it coming for us next, to see that its savagery would be incomparable to anything that had come for us before. Sometimes the dread was so heavy it felt like the war's spread would come as a relief. At least our wait would be over.

I say "we," I say "us," I say "our," as though we were, we are, a monolith in our opinions, in our experience. We, Lebanese, we, the waiters and the watchers. Which "we" do I mean? Which "us" am I purporting to speak for?

Not the people of South Lebanon, who were displaced under a rain of bombs from the first day. Not those who had assured themselves there would be no war on Lebanon—that it was too important to the Americans to destroy. Not those who said, "Good, let the Israelis take care of Hezbollah, let them do the dirty work." Not those who said, "Let the Israelis come, resistance at all costs." And certainly not those who endured this latest, most terrible assault on Lebanon—beginning with the unconscionable act of terrorism in September 2024, when thousands of pagers exploded across the country in broad daylight, blowing off hands, blinding eyes, killing 42 people, including 2 children, and injuring more than 4,000 civilians over two nightmarish days. An act of terrorism celebrated across the world for its "audacity" and "precision," since it had "only targeted Hezbollah operatives." But being an act of terrorism, it did exactly what it was meant to: it terrified people, made them suspicious of all their electronic devices, from cell phones to baby monitors.

But I was not there for any of this; I had left for Montreal, Canada, where my mother and brothers live, two weeks before. But I am not fully here, and certainly not physically there. This reality plays itself out in the most horrific way during those final twenty-four hours before the ceasefire went into effect on November 27.

As in 2006, the last hours before the ceasefire are the most savage, with Israel trying to cram as much death and destruction as it can into the final allotted hours of its reign of terror. It is still morning my time when the ceasefire is confirmed. Then, the long list of targets is disseminated on social media by the loathsome Avichay Adraee, the Arabic spokesperson for the IDF, who tweets threats at us in our own language. Israel barely gives people enough time to run from their homes or places of shelter. And then they bomb places that were never on the evacuation list in the first place.

I spend the entire day on the phone, frantically talking to friends and family, frantically texting across several different WhatsApp groups, trying to keep track of everyone I love. There are designated targets around our apartment. I speak to my then-husband, T, several times. I hear the drone, as always, ever-present in the background.

Bombs fall on the neighborhood where my cousin Hamra lives with her two teenage daughters. Traffic is at a standstill, and everyone is trying to run. She takes off on foot, their cat in tow. Hamra is threatened with an airstrike, right on the corner of my elderly uncle's street. We watch, in real time on one of the WhatsApp groups, as our dear friend A realizes that the bomb that fell in his neighborhood killed both his parents instantly.

It's impossible to breathe. I am there but not there. I hang up with Beirut. I call a friend in North America. I am here but not here, doubled over, howling with terror and grief, barely able to get coherent words out. I get another phone call from Beirut. I have to compose myself, hang up with North America. I cannot carry on like this with Beirut on the line. T again. I hear the airstrikes whistling and exploding around what was recently my home. The connection blinks out for a moment, and I shout his name until he comes back on the line. "I'm fine," he says, each time this happens. "But it was really close."

The ceasefire begins at 4:00 a.m. Beirut time, 9:00 p.m. East Coast time. It is only then that I can breathe again. I look around me. Suddenly, it seems absurd. All this time, I have been in this safe place, free to put away my phone and go about my day. A task that has been impossible for so many of us since October 7, 2023.

People talk about survivor's guilt. What I feel at this distance, in the aftermath of the war on Lebanon, or in the short lull before it begins again, and still, still watching the ever-escalating barbarism of the extermination of Gaza, is more than that. It is survivor's shame. I've been struggling to articulate the difference. It's seemingly minute but, in fact, vast. I suppose the best way to describe it is like this: Survivor's guilt is the sense that one is not worthy of having survived. Why them, why not me? Why do I deserve to live or emerge unscathed while they suffer? With survivor's shame, it is more like: I have managed to evade something that my loved ones did not. They have lived through something I have not, and thus I am unworthy of now counting myself among them. I will always, in this way, stand apart. I am exiled from this story of the people to whom I most dearly belong.

This is especially a struggle given that I have been asked, again and again, to talk and write about what's happening, the same way I have written and talked about all the many crises that have befallen my country over the last half-decade.

But this shame makes words difficult to come by. Or more precisely, it makes language, grammar, and approach difficult to pin down.

Yet, I am equally aware that war is fundamentally a collective trauma. And that there is a rhetorical and moral power in the "we," when it is honestly deployed, that is, for the widest "we," the most inclusive "us" possible.

Thus, this "us" is the story of Palestine, whose tragedy extends to Lebanon, whose loss extends to the entire Arab world—an entire region that has hardened into scar tissue around that central wound, that forcible gouging of Palestine from the map, the names of its towns and cities changed, its people massacred, its olive and orange groves burned, and its homes occupied—unwatered plants, unfinished food, and all.

And now, that "we" extends further outward still, to everyone watching this war, feeling disgraced by it on behalf of humanity itself.

# 18

# Why BDS Matters

*Omar Barghouti*
*Interviewed by Fatima Bhutto*

## 1. What is BDS and what led you to co-found this movement?

**OB** In 1985, I was a student at Columbia University in New York. I took part in the three-week peaceful blockade of Hamilton Hall demanding divestment from apartheid South Africa. The Black students–led protest, that quickly morphed into a mass movement supported by the Columbia community and many outside, was eventually recognized by the leadership of the anti-apartheid struggle, the African National Congress. Six months later, Columbia decided to fully divest from South Africa, becoming the first major US university to do so. Like everyone who participated in that fateful protest and thousands like it worldwide that contributed to dismantling political apartheid in South Africa, I shall always cherish that I was a tiny part of a massive righteous struggle that triumphed over a seemingly invincible regime of oppression.

The Boycott, Divestment and Sanctions (BDS) movement is, in a way, a globalized, Palestinian-led intifada, or uprising, aiming first and foremost to cut the links of state, corporate, and institutional complicity in Israel's decades-old regime of settler colonialism, apartheid, military occupation, and genocide. BDS is inspired by the South African anti-apartheid struggle and the US civil rights movement, and it is rooted in a century of Palestinian popular resistance first to British colonial rule and later to Zionist settler colonialism. As the struggle that ended apartheid in South Africa has shown, ending complicity in Israel's system of oppression, especially through the nonviolent tactics of BDS, is the most effective form of international solidarity with the Palestinian liberation struggle.

The cornerstone of this nonviolent movement was the BDS Call, launched in 2005 with the endorsement of the political, social, trade union, grassroots, and civil society entities representing the absolute majority of the Indigenous people of Palestine, in historic Palestine, as well as in exile. Led by the largest Palestinian coalition ever to exist, BDS aims at ending Israel's regime of military occupation and apartheid and upholding the right of Palestinian refugees to return home and receive reparations in accordance with relevant UN resolutions. These are the minimal conditions required in order for the Palestinian people to exercise its inalienable right to self-determination. BDS aims to contribute to the struggle to achieve Palestinian freedom, justice, and equality.

Anchored in the Universal Declaration of Human Rights, the BDS movement categorically opposes all forms of racism, including Islamophobia, antisemitism, and anti-Palestinian racism. It targets complicity, not identity.

The fact that I am a son of two refugees who dedicated their lives to the Palestinian liberation struggle has motivated me the most to play a key role in establishing the BDS movement.

**2. Apartheid is a legal term—I mean, it's not a matter of opinion whether Israel is practicing apartheid, is it? Can you speak to how Israel meets the legal definition of apartheid?**

**OB** Indeed, this is not a matter of opinion. Apartheid is a well-defined crime against humanity in international law. Major human rights organizations, the most prominent of which is Amnesty International, have published irrefutable legal evidence and analysis of Israel's apartheid against the Palestinian people. Even the usually timid and conservative Israeli human rights organization, B'Tselem, titled its own apartheid report "A Regime of Jewish Supremacy from the Jordan River to the Mediterranean Sea: This is Apartheid." The most important analysis of Israeli apartheid as "a tool of Zionist settler colonialism" was issued by the leading Palestinian human rights organization, Al-Haq, and endorsed by several others.

As a Jewish supremacist settler colony, Israel since its establishment on the ruins of the Palestinian homeland during the Nakba has enforced a regime of racial segregation that affords its Jewish citizens full rights while depriving its Indigenous Palestinian citizens of fundamental rights, not to mention its system of total segregation in the 1967 occupied Palestinian territory and its racist denial of the universally recognized rights of Palestinian refugees.

The ultimate blow to apartheid denial by Israel and its apologists in the colonial West, led by the United States, came in July 2024, when the International Court of Justice (ICJ) ruled that Israel's occupation of Gaza and the West Bank, including East Jerusalem, was entirely illegal and that "Israel's legislation and measures violate the international prohibition on racial segregation and apartheid," as stipulated in the International Convention on the Elimination of All Forms of Racial Discrimination (CERD), according to dozens of United Nations human rights experts.

### 3. How similar is apartheid in Israel to how it was practiced in South Africa?

**OB** South African apartheid—which formally began in 1948, the same year the Israeli settler-colonial apartheid regime came into existence—included "petty apartheid" laws, regulations, and conventions that segregated whites from Blacks in all public spaces and events as well as "grand apartheid laws that enforce racial domination at the economic and political levels." In the 1970s, under rising international pressure, South Africa's apartheid regime claimed to have relaxed some features of petty apartheid only to "consolidate and perpetuate white domination," as the UN Special Committee Against Apartheid said in a 1975 report.

As early as 1965, Palestinian diplomat and scholar Fayez Sayegh wrote that Zionist settler colonialism "has learned all the lessons which the various discriminatory regimes of white settler-states in Asia and Africa can teach it," adding, "For, whereas the Afrikaner apostles of apartheid in South Africa, for example, brazenly proclaim their sin, the Zionist practitioners of apartheid in Palestine beguilingly protest their innocence!" Building on this seminal work by Sayegh and a long record of Palestinian analyses, the BDS movement and its predecessor, the Palestinian Campaign for the Academic and Cultural Boycott of Israel (PACBI), have consistently analyzed Israel's regime as constituting settler colonialism, apartheid, and military occupation.

Israel's apartheid, far more sensitive than its South African counterpart to the state's international standing and to its propagandistic image as a "democracy," has mostly done away with petty apartheid, allowing mixing in restaurants, hospitals, and beaches, for the most part, while imposing laws and policies of racial domination, segregation, and colonial oppression against the entire Palestinian people, in the 1948 territory, in the 1967 occupied territory, as well as in exile.

**4. How wide-ranging is BDS? Can it be practiced just as a philosophy of consumption, as in "don't buy this" or "don't use this brand" or does it require a multi-pronged approach—boycotting academic institutions, cultural products, political abstention, etc., to be successful?**

OB As an integral form of Palestinian popular resistance and *the* most important form of international solidarity with the Palestinian liberation struggle, BDS is a set of principles and a set of strategic tools. It strives to reach a golden balance between ethical principles and strategic effectiveness, or *strategic radicalism*, in short. In other words, BDS campaigns are nonviolent, anti-racist, principled, and goal-oriented, and they adhere to the movement's operational principles of context-sensitivity, gradualness, and sustainability.

BDS targets complicity, not identity. It targets institutions, not individuals. It encompasses, inter alia, economic, financial, academic, cultural, and sports boycotts; military-security embargoes; divestment from—and excluding from contracts—corporations and banks that are complicit in Israel's war crimes, crimes against humanity, and now genocide; as well as targeted and lawful sanctions, including pressuring governments, local governments, regional bodies, etc., to fulfill their obligations under international law by ending all complicity with Israel's regime of oppression.

The BDS theory of change revolves around building power from the grassroots up to affect policy change. International law and ethical principles, after all, are necessary but woefully insufficient conditions for achieving justice and emancipation from colonial subjugation, as Palestinians have known for decades. Only more people power, grassroots power, especially channelled toward effective and strategic boycotts, divestment and lawful sanctions, can force the genocidal US-Israeli axis to stop the genocide, and can ultimately contribute to dismantling Israel's underlying regime of settler-colonial apartheid.

**5. It's impossible to ignore one of the main criticisms against your movement, levelled by Prime Minister Benjamin Netanyahu and Israel's defenders, that BDS is antisemitic. What's your response?**
**OB** The objective of this spurious and baseless smear is of course to deflect and distract from Israel's crimes against Palestinians, including apartheid and now genocide.

Regardless, given the immense influence Israel and the Zionist movement enjoy in mainstream Western political, cultural, academic, and media circles, Palestinians have no choice but to refute this propaganda head on.

Since its inception in 2005, the BDS movement has consistently rejected in word and in deed all forms of racism, including antisemitism, which is defined by the world's largest Jewish anti-Zionist organization, the US-based Jewish Voice for Peace, as "discrimination, targeting, violence, and dehumanizing stereotypes directed at Jews because they are Jewish," in harmony with mainstream definitions endorsed by hundreds of leading Jewish intellectuals and scholars, including world authorities on antisemitism and the Holocaust. Opposing, resisting, or boycotting Israel and Zionism have nothing to do with these standard definitions.

If a key feature of antisemitism is essentializing all Jews, considering them as a monolithic group or even a separate "race," Zionism and Israel, regardless of intent, are guilty of fanning the flames of antisemitism. By insisting on speaking for all Jews, treating them as if they were all part of the same "tribe," all "belonging" to Israel, calling on them to "go home" to Israel in the face of rising antisemitic attacks in their home countries, whether in France, the United States, or elsewhere, Israel and Zionism exacerbate antisemitism, which is a serious phenomenon most prominently and dangerously prevalent among white supremacists and far-right groups. Equating Israel with Jewry, holding all Jews responsible for Israel's crimes and apartheid policies, is a feature of today's rising antisemitism. Decoupling Jews from Israel, Jewishness from Zionism, or liberating Judaism from Zionism, as progressive Jewish intellectuals and activists advocate, therefore becomes an essential ingredient in the struggle against *real* anti-Jewish racism and for Jewish safety, well-being, and freedom from the shackles that come with Zionism.

Israel has faced great difficulty convincing anyone beyond its loyal lobby groups and anti-Palestinian racist partners that BDS was "antisemitic" mainly because of the movement's consistent, categorical, and public record of rejecting all forms of racism, and because of the significant worldwide Jewish support for BDS. In light of the legal warfare, or lawfare, strategy's failure to criminalize or quash BDS, Israel and its lobby groups have aggressively promoted a revisionist definition of antisemitism that aims "to shield Israel from being held accountable to universal standards of human rights and international law." Claiming that boycotting Israel is intrinsically antisemitic is not only baseless propaganda. It absurdly equates Israel with "all Jews." This is as bigoted as claiming that boycotting a self-defined Islamic state like Saudi Arabia, say, over its legalized discrimination against women or its war crimes in Yemen is tantamount to being Islamophobic.

As early as 2014, a poll by Israel lobby group J Street revealed that 46 percent of non-Orthodox Jewish American men under forty support a *full boycott of Israel*. Well before the current genocide, a 2021 poll by the Jewish Electorate Institute showed that 38 percent of Jewish Americans under forty agreed with the statement "Israel is an apartheid state," and 33 percent agreed that "Israel is committing genocide against the Palestinians." A 2022 poll shows that 16 percent of all Jewish Americans support BDS. They understand that there is nothing Jewish about Israel's siege, ethnic cleansing, massacres, land theft, occupation, apartheid, or genocide, and therefore there is nothing anti-Jewish in supporting BDS to end these crimes and systems of injustice.

Israel's own embrace of patent antisemites has irked even some of its staunch supporters.

In February 2019, for instance, the Israeli government hosted the prime ministers of the Czech Republic, Slovakia, and Hungary, all of whom had made public antisemitic and xenophobic statements. Defending Israel's partnership with such figures, Likud Knesset member Anat Berko has said, "They might be anti-Semites, but they're on our side." The following cartoon published in *Haaretz* on August 17, 2017, captures this cynical and pernicious Israeli revisionism:

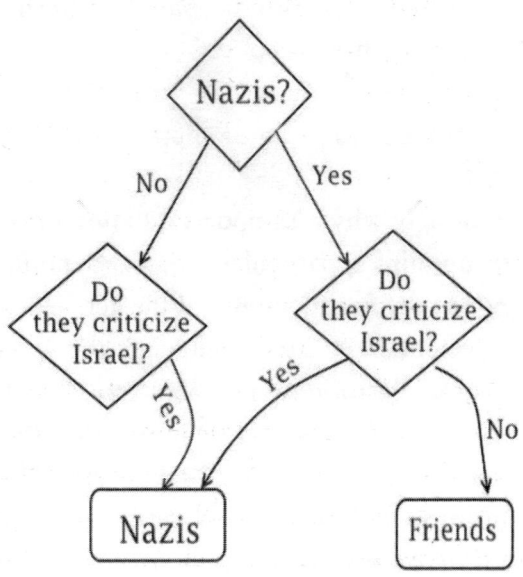

Understanding this revisionism and how it is manipulated to whitewash white supremacist and far-right antisemitism, in May 2019, when the German Bundestag passed a resolution smearing BDS as "antisemitic," more than 240 Jewish and Israeli scholars (many of them distinguished academics specializing in antisemitism, Jewish history, and the history of the Holocaust) were among the first to condemn the measure in a scathing statement. Crucially, they emphasized that the resolution did nothing to "advance the urgent fight against antisemitism." One day before the resolution passed, the German government released a study showing that 90 percent of the antisemitic—and other racist/xenophobic—attacks in Germany come from the far right, and a follow-up report placed that percentage at 96 percent. Such attacks come from the voter pool of the patently antisemitic, far-right party, Alternative für Deutschland, that has proposed an even more anti-democratic resolution outlawing the BDS movement completely but failed to get wide support for it.

**6. Can you speak to why it's important to boycott Israeli academic institutions in particular? It's worth noting that we are speaking in the fifteenth month of the genocide.**

**OB** On September 18, 2024, following the International Court of Justice's historic ruling about Israel's illegal occupation and apartheid system, dozens of UN human rights experts urged states to fully comply with the ICJ ruling by adopting measures to, inter alia, "Cancel or suspend economic relationships, trade agreements, and *academic relations* with

Israel that may contribute to its unlawful presence and apartheid regime in the occupied Palestinian territory." [Emphasis added.]

Israel's ongoing genocide, according to UN human rights experts, has included "domicide, urbicide, scholasticide, medicide, cultural genocide and, more recently, ecocide." Israel has destroyed every single Palestinian university in Gaza and hundreds of schools, killing educators and students in shocking numbers, prompting the heads of fifteen Palestinian universities to call for isolating Israeli universities worldwide. Despite the repression and in response to Palestinian calls, tens of thousands of academics now support the academic boycott of Israel.

Israeli universities have not only supported this genocide but have for decades been an indispensable pillar in Israel's regime of oppression, as meticulously documented in the book *Towers of Ivory and Steel* by Israeli anthropologist Maya Wind. Wind has also exposed their complicity in Israel's ongoing Gaza genocide. Israeli universities have for decades systematically provided the military-intelligence establishment with indispensable research—on weapons technologies and military doctrines, archaeology, demography, geography, hydrology, psychology, philosophy, among other disciplines. Some universities, like Hebrew University, have also themselves built illegal colonial facilities and dormitories in the occupied Palestinian territory.

One stark example is Tel Aviv University's Institute for National Security Studies, which takes credit for the development of the so-called Dahiya Doctrine, or doctrine of disproportionate force, that is adopted by the Israeli Army and which calls for "the destruction of the national [civilian] infrastructure, and intense suffering among the [civilian] population," as a means of defeating an otherwise "impossible" to defeat non-statal resistance. What we're seeing in Gaza and to a lesser extent in the West Bank and Lebanon manifests the Dahiya Doctrine at work.

Israel's scholasticide, a term coined by Karma Nabulsi, a prominent Palestinian scholar at Oxford University, did not begin in October 2023, however, but goes back to the 1948 ethnic cleansing of Palestine, the Nakba. An Israeli researcher's dissertation, for instance, reveals that during and immediately after the Nakba, tens of thousands of books, stolen from Palestinian homes, schools, and libraries in Jerusalem, Jaffa, Haifa, Safad, and elsewhere, were plundered and many of them destroyed by Zionist—and later Israeli—militias.

In the first few weeks of the Palestinian Intifada, or popular uprising (1987–93), Israel shut down all Palestinian universities (some, like Birzeit, for several consecutive years), and then it closed all 1,194 Palestinian schools in the occupied West Bank (including East Jerusalem) and Gaza. Next came the kindergartens. Eventually, every educational institution in the occupied Palestinian territory was forcibly closed. This prompted Palestinians to build an "illegal network" of underground schools.

Based on all this complicity, the Palestinian Campaign for the Academic and Cultural Boycott of Israel (PACBI), a key part of the Palestinian-led BDS movement, has called since 2004 for the boycott of complicit Israeli universities (and cultural institutions). BDS targets institutions, not individuals.

In August, a legal opinion published by international law experts at the University of Antwerp said that universities, as "organs of society endowed with the responsibility to teach and educate," must "avoid aiding and assisting the commission of serious breaches of peremptory norms of international law created by Israel's illegal presence in the Occupied Palestinian Territory, and address such aid and assistance when it occurs." Affirming the complicity of Israeli universities, the legal opinion concludes by calling on universities to: "End all collaborations with academic and other institutions directly or indirectly implicated in the violations of international law, international human rights law and international humanitarian law in Gaza and in the Occupied Palestinian territories, more generally."

Complicity, after all, is absolutely incompatible with any notion of "neutrality" that some university rectors and academics fallaciously claim.

The student-led uprising in solidarity with Palestine on campuses worldwide, particularly in the US and Europe, must be understood in this context. It is a bright, inspiring sign of Palestine's South Africa moment, as the solidarity movement is reaching a tipping point in the struggle for Palestinian liberation.

**7. I heard you say once that what we are witnessing being done to Gaza has dangerous implications for the entire world and that it's a fatal miscalculation to see Israel's warfare as only a Palestinian issue—can you elaborate on how so?**

OB If many in the world today see Palestinian rights as the "litmus test for human rights," in the words of South African jurist and former UN Special Rapporteur for Human Rights John Dugard from many years ago, support for Palestinian liberation, especially through BDS tactics, has become a litmus test for not just *meaningful* and *impactful* international solidarity with the Palestinian liberation struggle, but also for progressive politics generally.

Palestinians are not the first people to be subjected to genocide. Unfortunately, we may not be the last either. But the US-Israeli genocide against 2.3 million Palestinians in Gaza is the world's first *live-streamed* genocide. Armed, funded, and shielded from accountability by the colonial West, Israel is in fact displaying what even the meek UN Secretary-General calls "total impunity." It has not only exterminated tens of thousands of Palestinians in Gaza, and in a few weeks killed thousands in Lebanon and occupied more lands in Syria, it is simultaneously bulldozing the very tenets of international law just as ruthlessly as it had bulldozed hundreds of Palestinian villages during the 1947–9 Nakba—the planned ethnic cleansing of a majority of the Indigenous people of Palestine to establish Israel as a settler colony.

Unless stopped, Israel, enabled by the colonial West, will usher in a "might makes right" era unseen since World

War II. The already flawed Western liberal democracy would disintegrate into what the Congolese American sociologist Pierre van den Berghe calls "herrenvolk democracy," democracy only for the master race, as Israel has always been, according to Israeli historian Ilan Pappé.

As early as October 2023, days into Israel's genocidal attack in Gaza, Colombian President Gustavo Petro warned of the "unprecedented rise of fascism, and therefore, to the death of democracy and freedom." "Gaza," he said, "is just the first experiment in considering us all disposable." Giving us a taste of what such a dystopian future may look like, in 2024, US Secretary of State Antony Blinken said, "If you're not at the table in the international system, you're going to be on the menu." Clearly, not only Israel is on trial at the International Court of Justice (ICJ); so is the entire Western-dominated international legal system. As international law scholar Mohsen al Attar puts it, "*South Africa v. Israel* will achieve what no anti-colonial movement ever could: a reckoning between international law and settler colonialism, starting with Euroamerica's darling in the Levant."

Keenly cognizant of all this, oppressed communities worldwide increasingly view the complicity of states in maintaining Israel's live-streamed genocide and underlying, decades-old regime of systematic oppression of Palestinians as undermining the very legitimacy of the law-based international order, which in turn undermines their own domestic struggles for justice. This has pressured governments worldwide to express the same visceral concern for humanity's fate should Israel, with US and European support, succeed in fatally injuring the UN and burying decades of international law together with the tens of thousands of Palestinian children, men, and women that it has murdered in Gaza.

For example, during the UN General Assembly in September 2024 that upheld the implementation of the ICJ ruling about the illegality of Israel's entire presence in the occupied Palestinian territory, including East Jerusalem, a rising number of states not only expressed support for Palestinians facing Israel's ongoing genocide but also warned about Western hypocrisy undermining the entire system of international law and multilateralism. Indonesia's foreign minister put it succinctly when she said she brought "the voice of the Global South," the spirit of the Bandung Conference, in calling on states to *not* "bury the Principles of the UN Charter and international law under the rubble of double standards, trust deficit, and zero-sum game."

Already, incoming US President Donald Trump is threatening to annex Canada, Greenland, and the Panama Canal to the United States, hinting at resorting to military action to achieve these brazen goals.

An unintended consequence of this US-Israeli savagery in eroding Palestinian lives and livelihoods and with them the pillars of international law is the dramatic shift in international civil society's understanding of Israel's regime of oppression as including apartheid, a crime against humanity under international law, and, crucially, in mainstreaming calls for targeted and lawful sanctions to bring an end to Israel's decades-old violations of Palestinian rights and international law.

**8. The Israeli regime of oppression did not begin on October 7. How has BDS changed since the genocide began?**

OB Israel's genocide in Gaza stems from and must be situated in the context of seventy-six years of its regime of settler colonialism and apartheid against the Indigenous Palestinian people, which have included what Israeli historian Ilan Pappé has characterized as an "incremental genocide." This was well-documented and articulated by leading international law experts who represented South Africa in the genocide case against Israel at the ICJ in January 2024 and, more recently, by the UN Special Rapporteur for Human Rights in the occupied Palestinian territory, Francesca Albanese, in her October 2024 report to the UN General Assembly titled "Genocide as Colonial Erasure."

Over the last two decades, the BDS movement has planted the seeds of effective and principled solidarity with the Palestinian struggle for freedom, justice, and equality by building a massive network worldwide, supported by trade unions, farmers' coalitions, as well as racial, social, gender, and climate justice movements, together representing tens of millions, and laying the foundations for cutting complicity in Israel's crimes. BDS has over the years played a significant role in the divestment of giant sovereign funds in Norway, Luxembourg, the Netherlands, New Zealand, and elsewhere from complicit companies and banks.

With the onslaught of Israel's genocide in October 2023, while none of us in the BDS movement was prepared for the unspeakable brutality that would eventually unfold, BDS foundations and tools have proven to be exceptionally effective in exposing the crimes, raising awareness about the criminals, and, most crucially, shining a light on the proper courses of action that need to be taken globally to end state, corporate, and institutional complicity in Israel's genocide and underlying apartheid. During this ongoing genocide, the B and the D in BDS have grown exponentially, but the most qualitative change in the movement's impact has been in the S—lawful and targeted sanctions have begun to mainstream.

When the BDS movement first called for a comprehensive military embargo on Israel, for instance, states were too terrified of US wrath to even consider it. Now, the global majority at the UN General Assembly supports it, as evidenced in the UNGA resolution enacting the ICJ ruling about Israel's illegal occupation. In July 2024, over thirty UN human rights experts called on states to respect the ICJ ruling that Israel's occupation is illegal by imposing sanctions and a military embargo on Israel. In November 2024, Turkey launched an initiative for imposing a military embargo on Israel, garnering the endorsement of over fifty-two states so far, including permanent and non-permanent Security Council members. The initiative was also adopted by the joint summit of the Organization of Islamic Cooperation (OIC) and the League of Arab States.

When the BDS movement first called in 2005 for meaningful, impactful forms of accountability—including lawful, targeted sanctions—as fulfillment of states' legal obligations to refrain from recognizing, aiding, or assisting Israel's violations of peremptory norms of international law, very few states would even consider the "S" in BDS. Today, holding Israel accountable for its atrocity crimes by, inter alia, imposing a comprehensive, two-way military-security embargo on it as well as sanctions has become much more acceptable among many states, despite the unprecedented level of bullying and intimidation from the colonial West, led by the United States.

Since the beginning of Israel's genocide in Gaza in October 2023, the BDS movement and its many partners globally have played a significant, and sometimes decisive role, in pressuring national and local governments worldwide to end or scale back complicity with Israel's regime of oppression. For example, in November 2024, the Organization of Islamic Cooperation, South Africa, and Belize, among others, called for the reconstitution of the UN Special Committee Against Apartheid, a key demand of the BDS movement since 2020. Also in November, the African Commission on Human and People's Rights responded to BDS calls and adopted the first resolution on Palestine in twenty-four years calling on African states to end complicity and ensure accountability. Turkey has suspended trade with Israel, and following tireless campaigning by BDS Turkey, six Turkish municipalities have ended their sister city protocol with Israel.

Thirty-five Basque city councils have adopted motions calling for sanctions, including a two-way military embargo, against Israel and the suspension of diplomatic and institutional relations with it. The Cheyenne River Sioux Tribe of South Dakota (US) has endorsed the BDS Call "in solidarity with the indigenous people of Palestine." The Belgian municipality of Ixelles has suspended its twinning agreement with the Israeli Regional Council of Megiddo. In Australia, the City of Canterbury-Bankstown Council has passed a BDS resolution, and the Inner West Council, Sydney has passed a motion on procurement to comply with BDS, while in the United States, Alameda, CA, has become the first county in the US to ban all investments in weapons companies and fossil fuels. Nelson City, Aotearoa (New Zealand) has become the fourth in the country to end its ties with illegal Israeli settlements.

Trade union federations from South Africa to Norway and from Brazil and India to the UK, France, and Canada have endorsed BDS. IndustriALL Global Union, a global union federation that represents 50 million workers in 140 countries in the mining, energy and manufacturing sectors, has endorsed BDS, becoming by far the largest trade union body to do so. The trade union federation of Norway, LO, representing a million workers, has pressured the Norwegian pension fund, the largest sovereign fund in the world, to divest its entire holding of approximately $500 million of Israel Bonds. Major Indian trade unions representing tens of millions of workers have demanded of the Indian government to cancel an agreement to "export" Indian workers to Israel to replace Palestinian workers, urging workers to boycott Israeli products and to not handle Israeli cargo. Dockworkers' unions in Belgium, India, Catalonia, Italy, Greece, Turkey, California, and South Africa have taken actions against Israeli ships or arms shipments to Israel. IAATW, an international worker-led alliance of app-based transport workers' unions with 100,000 members from over twenty-seven countries and six continents, has decided to boycott Chevron-branded gas stations. Seven major US unions representing 6 million workers have called on the Biden administration to halt all military funding to Israel, in an unprecedented development in the United States.

In the corporate world, McDonald's has recently admitted the significant impact of our BDS campaign against it, while US tech giant Intel has halted its construction of a new $25 billion factory in Israel. According to Intel insiders, the BDS movement's #BoycottIntel fact sheet has played a considerable role in convincing key Intel shareholders, managers, and workers that the company's plans to invest $25 billion in a "war zone" was not only unethical and illegal but also utterly irresponsible from a fiduciary/financial angle as well. During Israel's ongoing Gaza genocide, more than 80 percent of Israeli start-ups have suffered damages, with over 50 percent of start-ups left with less than six months of cash. "Angel investors" dropped by 75 percent in 2023, and growth capital investing in Israeli companies was down 32 percent year-over-year in Q1 2024. As prominent Israeli economists are admitting, Israel's once vaunted high tech is collapsing.

Israeli high tech in general is nosediving and foreign investment is drying up, prompting the BDS movement since early 2023 to coin the hashtag #ShutDownNation, eventually used by the *Financial Times* and even by anti-Netanyahu Israeli demonstrators prior to the genocide. The current "spiral of collapse" of the Israeli economy, as 130 leading Israeli economists have characterized it, is mainly due to the genocide and the associated "security" and financial risks, but it is also partly due to BDS campaigning. "BDS and boycotts have changed Israel's global trade landscape," admitted Avi Balashnikov, Chairman of the Israel Export Institute.

The academic, cultural, and sports boycotts of Israel, which target institutions, have spread across the world. Most recently, 1,000 writers, including Nobel Prize laureates, Pulitzer Prize winners, and Sally Rooney, "have joined history's largest cultural boycott against Israel's publishing industry." Within weeks, thousands more have joined them.

City councils, especially in Europe and Latin America, have taken decisive measures against Israeli apartheid and companies supporting it or adopted ethical procurement policies.

**9. At the same time as BDS is successful—ethically and on the ground in terms of effect— you're being met with global crackdowns. Can you speak to anti-BDS legislation and how these bills are being used as templates to go after other progressive movements?**

**OB** Despite its military, diplomatic, and economic power, and despite its dominant influence in the US government and, by extension, in the UK and European Union, Israel's regime of military occupation, settler colonialism, and apartheid still views the Palestinian-led global BDS movement as a "strategic threat" to its system of injustice, waging a protracted war against the movement accordingly. Israel's full enlistment of Washington, London, Berlin, Paris, and Brussels, among many other Western powers, in its war on the BDS movement for Palestinian rights is the strongest indicator of the movement's impact on its regime of military occupation, settler colonialism, and apartheid, and of its failure to crush the movement.

The fact that high-ranking figures in the Biden administration declared war on BDS soon after the January 2021 inauguration confirms what Palestinians and progressive supporters of Palestinian rights had predicted—that US complicity in Israel's war on BDS would continue, albeit couched in rhetorical respect for constitutional free speech. That was also a harbinger of the Biden administration's later full partnership in Israel's Gaza genocide. But how did BDS, a nonviolent movement, become such a "strategic" challenge to Israel, a country with immense military power, including a nuclear arsenal; economic strength—despite its seemingly "spiral" decline and risk of "collapse"—sustained by billions of dollars in aid from (and favorable trade regimens with) the United States, Germany, and other Western countries; and decades-long impunity for its egregious violations of international law?

BDS quickly became a target of attack by the Israeli government and its allies in the United Kingdom, the United States, and elsewhere. To cite just one recent example, the Trump administration notified Kenya in September 2020 that it could forget about a free trade agreement with the world's largest economy unless Nairobi discouraged "politically motivated actions to boycott, divest from, and sanction Israel" and eliminated "state-sponsored, unsanctioned foreign boycotts of Israel" as well as "non-tariff barriers on

Israeli goods, services, or other commerce imposed on
Israel." The Democratic Party has systematically resisted
meaningful justice and reparations for Indigenous nations
and Black Americans following centuries of colonialism and
enslavement. The recent Democratic National Convention
has reaffirmed the party's support for the Biden administration's partnership in Israel's Gaza genocide, insisting on
unconditionally arming Israel, and attacking the BDS movement in its platform.

Germany is applying McCarthyite repression against
anyone who dares to endorse BDS or advocate for the
UN-stipulated rights of the Indigenous Palestinian people.
The Jewish American historian Susan Neiman has described
the atmosphere in Germany as "philosemitic McCarthyism,"
while the columnist Daniel Bax argued that "Germany must
decide between *Staatsräson* and international law." In
November 2024, the Lemkin Institute for Genocide Prevention
condemned Germany's repression and complicity in Israel's
genocide, saying:

> Many of us believed that Germany had really made strides
> in recognizing its genocidal past, at least in terms of the
> Holocaust, and was a stronger democracy for it. We were
> wrong.
>
> Genocide begets genocide begets genocide. The
> German state and German elites have clearly learned
> nothing from their history. They continue to persecute
> Jews without so much as a moment of hesitation if it serves
> their raison d'etat. Now they have added Palestinians as

new victims of German genocide—Palestinians who inherited the consequences of Germany's crimes!

This raises serious questions about what should be done with serial genocide states. Can genocidal societies ever transform away from their genocidal pasts?

While Israel celebrates its enormous, some argue unparalleled, influence in the United States, it is missing the growing undercurrent of resentment and apprehension that these McCarthyite tactics are creating. A University of Maryland poll published in 2020, for instance, revealed that 72 percent of all Americans (80 percent of Democrats) were opposed to anti-BDS laws because they infringe on freedom of speech. Among those who had heard of the movement, 42 percent of Americans (77 percent of Democrats) supported the statement that "BDS is a legitimate, peaceful way of opposing Israeli occupation of the Palestinian territories. Inspired by the South African anti-apartheid movement, BDS urges action to pressure Israel to comply with international law. Opposing Israeli policy does not equal antisemitism."

In a major blow to Israel's lawfare efforts in Europe, the European Court of Human Rights (ECHR) ruled unanimously in June 2020 that the highest French court's 2015 criminal conviction of BDS activists advocating nonviolent boycotts of Israeli goods violated article 10 (freedom of expression clause) of the European Convention on Human Rights. The ECHR ruled that the boycott call to end Israel's decades-long violations of Palestinian rights does not constitute incitement to discrimination, hate, or anti-Jewish bigotry. Since 2016, and in a decisive defeat for Israel's legal war on BDS in Europe and beyond, the European Union, the governments of Sweden, Ireland, and Netherlands, as well as leading international human rights organizations such as Amnesty International and the International Federation for Human Rights (FIDH) have all defended the right to boycott Israel as a matter of freedom of speech.

### 10. Is it truly possible to end all complicity in Israel's crimes?

**OB** It is not necessary to end all complicity in Israel's crimes against Palestinians in order to help dismantle its decades-old regime of settler colonialism, apartheid, and military occupation. South African apartheid, after all, was abolished as a political system with the first democratic, inclusive elections in 1994 not because all international complicity had ended, but because a tipping point on the path to ending complicity had been reached, giving enormous impetus to the internal resistance to dismantle apartheid.

Unlike South Africa under apartheid, the Israeli settler colony does not control massive deposits of precious metals and natural resources that the global capitalist system critically needs. Apartheid Israel's main exports, military and "security" (including cybersecurity) materiel and tech products incubated in the military, are tools of death, repression, and mass oppression, tested on Palestinian, Lebanese, and other Arab bodies. It also exports polished diamonds that are sourced under conditions of human rights violations, severe exploitation, and corruption in African countries and increasingly polished in India!

Ideological commitment to Zionism and Israel as a Zionist state has always played a hidden yet very prominent role in driving foreign investment in Israel, while veiled behind propaganda claims of Israel's high-tech "might." Many leading US tech companies have made large acquisitions of Israeli start-ups or invested immense sums in Israel's economy partly based on this ideological commitment to Zionism, as media reports are increasingly revealing. In December 2023, over two months into Israel's #GazaGenocide, Intel's then Christian Zionist CEO announced plans for investing $25 billion in a factory miles away from Gaza, defying not just international law and ethical principles but basic financial and fiduciary responsibility. Following shareholders' pressure, the plan was scrapped.

The founders and leaders of Sequoia Capital, a giant venture capital firm, also display not just severe anti-Palestinian racism but also a blinding commitment to Zionism. The firm is planning to reinvest in Israel, after years of a hiatus, well into its live-streamed genocide and despite the downgrading of Israel's economy and economic prospects by the world's leading credit rating agencies, the "spiral of collapse" of its economy, as its own top economists are warning, among other factors that have convinced almost all rational investors to pull out or stay away.

All these and many similar factors make Israel's economy, as the last fifteen months have shown, far more vulnerable to global pressure than apartheid South Africa's ever was. This is what makes BDS strategies the most effective form of international solidarity with the Palestinian struggle, even in the economic and financial domains.

**11. You must get this all the time, but what can we as individuals do? If I as one person boycott Israeli cultural festivals and Moroccan Oil hair products, how am I furthering the struggle to end complicity?**

OB Boycotting is not about feeling good but about actually making a dent in the wall of international complicity, and for this reason it has to be not just principled, anti-racist, and intersectional but also goal-oriented, strategic, incremental, and impactful. Also, to be effective, it has to be collective. Whether one is engaged in consumer, academic, cultural, sports, or any other form of boycott or divestment campaigns, one has to work within strategic groups that can build people power to affect change.

The overarching operational principles that guide BDS campaigning in all realms are: gradualness (incrementalism in building power to achieve the ultimate goals); sustainability (sustaining victories and building on them to move forward); and context-sensitivity (adapting tactics to optimally suit the political-cultural context).

As far as grassroots consumer boycotts go, and as the most recently updated "Guide to BDS Boycott & Pressure Corporate Priority Targeting" states, "People of conscience around the world are rightfully shattered, enraged, and sometimes feeling powerless about Israel's Gaza genocide, armed, funded, and shielded from accountability by the colonial West, led by the United States. Many feel compelled to boycott all products and services of companies tied in any way to Israel. The question is how to make boycotts most effective and impactful in holding corporations accountable for their complicity in the suffering of Palestinians."

The BDS movement has adopted the historically proven method of targeted boycotts inspired by the South African anti-apartheid movement, the US civil rights movement, the Indian and the Irish anti-colonial struggles, among others. BDS strategically focuses on a relatively smaller number of carefully selected companies and products for maximum impact. The movement's boycott target-selection criteria are: the level of complicity (based on accurate, convincing research that proves complicity); intersectionality (cross-movement relevance of the targeted company); brand recognition and media appeal (helps reaching a wider audience); and potential for success.

BDS campaigns ideally target companies that play a clear and direct role in Israel's crimes against Palestinians, as well as in violating the rights of other peoples and communities, and where there is real potential for achieving the campaign's goals. This is how the BDS movement has successfully forced large corporations like G4S, Veolia, Orange, Puma, and Pillsbury, among others, to end their complicity in Israel's grave human rights violations and crimes. Through strategic and context-sensitive boycott and divestment campaigns, as well as well-thought-out shareholder strategies and direct-action tactics, the BDS movement forces corporations to end their complicity in Israeli apartheid and war crimes against

Palestinians, sending a very powerful message to hundreds of other complicit companies that unless they end their own complicity, their "time will come."

As an intersectional movement that connects Palestinian liberation with racial, Indigenous, social, gender, and climate justice struggles, the BDS movement also recommends prioritizing the boycott of companies that are targets of mobilizations in other struggles of the oppressed. We recommend, where applicable, adopting an ethical investment policy or a universal human rights–based investment screen, to prevent investments in all companies complicit in human rights violations *anywhere*.

## 12. Lastly, how do you see the next few years shaping up? And how can people heartbroken and outraged by the genocide be of use practically?

OB In the face of history's first live-streamed genocide armed, funded, and justified by the so-called "liberal democracies" of the West, it is only natural for people of conscience worldwide to feel almost uncontainable rage, grief, and even fear. Some have fallen despondent, complaining of "genocide fatigue." But it is crucial to remember that Palestinians, especially in Gaza, do not have the luxury of "genocide fatigue," as Israel continues to massacre, starve, burn, thirst, and forcibly displace hundreds of thousands of our people.

Palestinians have never given up hope in our decades-old resistance to Israel's ruthless regime of oppression. This hope is rooted in our people's steadfastness, insistence on our existence in our homeland, in freedom, justice, equality, and dignity, and in the inspiring growth of the global solidarity movement's impact.

As the British Pakistani writer Nadeem Aslam says, "Despair has to be earned. I personally have not done all I can to change things. I haven't yet earned the right to despair." Unless one has earned that right, one has to channel their grief and rage into more effective organizing, strategizing, coalescing, hoping, acting, building people power to end complicity in one's sphere of relative influence, for Palestinian liberation and for ensuring that no racialized or vulnerable community is ever again put on the "menu" of imperial powers.

*Omar Barghouti donated his contributor fee to UNRWA.*

# Gaza Reflections

*Joe Sacco*

# 19
# Uprising on a University Campus
*Maryam Iqbal*

The absence of fear. This is my most vivid memory from our encampment. For the first time, I witnessed an unprecedented collective courage—the willingness to sacrifice. It was a turning point, a moment of realization: We had ignited something far greater than any of us. Thousands of students, united by a shared understanding, stood with us, resolute in their conviction that normalcy cannot coexist with the genocide unfolding in Gaza.

At this moment, there was still a distinction between the core group of about sixty students within the encampment, who had pledged themselves to remain in this encampment at the risk of possible arrest and disciplinary action, and the broader student body, who saw it as their duty to shield and support us from the outside. This dynamic, though marked by different roles, was unified by a shared purpose: to protect what we had built and to stand unwavering in the face of threats.

Outside the gates—barred to non-Columbia affiliates, as they always were during our protests—local groups like Palestinian Youth Movement, Within Our Lifetime, and many others were picketing tirelessly through every waking hour and into the night. For thirty-eight hours, we stood together, fortified by the strength of our community, holding off the NYPD. In those hours, I felt an unparalleled love for the Palestine organizing space in NYC, a love born from the unwavering solidarity and shared purpose that bound us together.

Earlier, as the final tent was secured around 3:00 a.m. and the last pieces of our protest art were placed across the lawn, the gravity of the moment struck me. I knelt before a tent adorned with a banner reading LIBERATED ZONE and snapped a photo, instinctively comparing it to an image from the 1968 protests at Columbia featuring the same banner. We had often told the student body that our movement was a continuation of the Vietnam War protests and the divestment campaigns against apartheid South Africa. The visual parallel between the two LIBERATED ZONE banners—one from 1968, the other from 2024—captured that legacy. And this is how we launched our encampment to the world.

As a Kashmiri Muslim woman born and raised in the United States, I have long grappled with the realities of systemic racism and Islamophobia. From an early age, books became my compass, helping me navigate my identity and understand the larger forces shaping the world around me. This journey of discovery deepened as I delved into postcolonial theory, immersing myself in seminal works such as Edward Said's *Orientalism* and *Culture and Imperialism*, Frantz Fanon's *The Wretched of the Earth*, and Noam Chomsky's

*Manufacturing Consent.* These texts unveiled a critical truth for me: Racism and Islamophobia are not merely social prejudices but are integral components of imperialist structures designed to justify and perpetuate colonial violence. They exposed how these ideologies serve a more insidious purpose—manufacturing consent for the annihilation of entire peoples, an atrocity we are bearing witness to today in Gaza.

When I applied to Columbia, I made no attempt to hide my identity or convictions. My personal statement centered on the murder of Palestinian journalist Shireen Abu Akleh by Israeli Occupation Forces in May 2022—a tragedy that deeply affected me after years of admiring her work. I made my identity and values explicit for a reason: For me, a crucial, non-negotiable factor in selecting a college was the presence of academic freedom. I sought an institution where open discourse could thrive, rejecting places that stifled voices advocating for Palestine. Columbia stood out as a place of intellectual freedom and debate—a campus that embodied contradictions. I was aware that it hosted a major Zionist presence, bolstered by its Tel Aviv Dual Degree program. Yet it also housed the Center for Palestine Studies and a legacy of academics central to the discourse on Palestinian liberation whom I looked up to immensely, including Edward Said, Rashid Khalidi, Lila Abu-Lughod, and Joseph Massad.

I dared to believe that an application written with unflinching honesty would serve as a litmus test, ensuring that I would find an institution that valued me for who I am. I could not have been more mistaken.

After October 7, Columbia University, like many institutions across the United States, swiftly issued emails expressing explicit sympathy for Israel. The message from Columbia's School of General Studies Dean extended condolences to "students who are reservists in the IDF," while obfuscating Palestinian resistance as "terrorism." In stark contrast, the Students for Justice in Palestine chapters at Columbia, Harvard, and other universities issued statements that contextualized Palestinian resistance within the broader framework of decades of occupation and systemic violence.

The backlash was immediate and unprecedented.

Doxxing trucks began to circulate—massive digital billboards mounted on trucks, broadcasting the names and faces of student activists alongside incendiary labels like "Columbia's leading antisemites." At first, these trucks targeted Harvard, where they circled for hours around campus. At Columbia, we took it as a warning and implemented strict operational security. We concealed our identities with masks and all-black clothing, avoided openly affiliating ourselves with Students for Justice in Palestine, and took every precaution to protect ourselves. We understood the risks; those trucks were already scouring campuses, and it was only a matter of time before they came for us. And they did. Unable to identify the core organizers of our chapter as a result of our precautions, they indiscriminately targeted members of Columbia's Muslim Students Association (MSA) and Arab Students Association (Turath), doxxing entire student boards.

It escalated from there. Muslim women had their hijabs ripped off and were spat on in broad daylight. Zionists yelled

"ISIS" at random Muslim and brown students on campus. At our first protest in October 2023, a Columbia staff member openly declared that he wanted us all to die, and this was broadcast on the student radio, WKCR. Handwritten death threats were discovered scattered around campus. A Columbia student publicly shared a plan for "nuke maps" of Gaza, openly advocated for the execution of all Palestinian men aged twelve and older, suggested placing women in "reeducation camps," and proposed adopting Palestinian children out to new families. This genocidal rhetoric was just the beginning. Instances of overt hatred and violence from Zionist students and faculty continued to proliferate, yet they were met with silence from the administration and the media alike.

The role of the main newspaper on campus, *Columbia Spectator*, in fueling this environment was particularly disturbing. The paper published an op-ed that repeated the debunked, orientalist lie about babies being beheaded on October 7—a malicious falsehood that had already been weaponized to manufacture consent for the annihilation of Palestinians through mainstream media. While I was already horrified to witness outlets like CNN spread such blatant atrocity propaganda, repeated by even Joe Biden himself, it was even more appalling to see the *Columbia Spectator*—an independently funded, student-run newspaper I worked for at the time—reproduce these lies. In that moment, I became acutely aware of the power of propaganda and the unsettling reality that the average person was deeply vulnerable to such falsehoods, which would continue to disseminate with impunity through mainstream Western media.

To watch the unfolding genocide in Gaza on our screens every day while simultaneously facing unprecedented hostility and violence on campus was almost unbearable. The early days of this horror were marked by relentless attacks on our movement, our identities, and our very humanity. We found ourselves without the space to grieve, as each new day brought a new death toll in Gaza and new forms of psychological warfare from Zionist forces on our campus. It was a double assault: one against the people of Gaza and one against anyone who dared to demand their survival.

Despite the relentless pressure, we persisted, organizing weekly protests to sustain the energy within the student body and keep the genocide in Gaza at the forefront of public awareness. This effort was a collective endeavor that stretched far beyond individual campuses or even the United States—it was a global movement. We recognized that we could not allow this momentum to wane; our cause was too urgent, the stakes were too high, the level of attention on Palestine was at levels we could not afford to lose—rivaling even the global outcry seen during the 2021 Sheikh Jarrah protests.

Despite our efforts to adhere to every guideline set for recognized student organizations, new obstacles were systematically placed in our path. Pro-Palestinian students were threatened with academic probation, with some facing the loss of financial aid. Meanwhile, Zionist students continued to dox and threaten us on campus. On one particularly harrowing occasion, Israeli Occupation Forces (IOF) soldiers launched a chemical attack during a protest. Two individuals, later identified as IOF soldiers, had disguised themselves in keffiyehs to blend in with the crowd. They sprayed a chemical substance that some Palestinian students later recognized as similar to "skunk"—a notorious crowd control weapon used in the West Bank by Israeli soldiers—into the gathered students. The effects were immediate and severe: intense coughing, eye irritation, disrupted menstrual cycles, and respiratory distress. Several students, myself included, required hospitalization.

The surveillance and crackdowns were no longer subtle— they were increasingly dangerous and severe. One incident stands out; a group of us attended a Within Our Lifetime protest in Washington Square Park. As we made our way to the subway, we noticed members of the NYPD's counterterrorism unit trailing us. They shadowed our every movement, getting off at the same stops and transfers, their eyes fixed on us as they communicated openly over their walkie-talkies, without even the pretense of discretion. It was a stark reminder of the extensive reach of the state's surveillance apparatus—not only embedded in our academic lives but extending into every corner of our daily existence.

The Columbia administration failed to grasp that their constant and severe repression had a radicalizing effect on the wider student body. But despite the consistent protests week after week, our efforts began to feel repetitive and futile, only revealing new forms of administrative repression each time. We realized that we needed to channel this mounting energy into something more impactful. Since January, we had been quietly planning a larger escalation. We sought an action that would be highly visible, centrally located on campus, one that could politically educate and agitate, build a sense of community, and most crucially, involve a physical occupation of space. We knew that this action would need to carry a clear message: we would refuse to leave until our central demand was met.

At midnight, as rain drenched the campus and we neared the twenty-four-hour mark of our encampment, something unexpected happened—a spontaneous protest erupted. Spontaneously, hundreds of students, acting on their own volition, began chanting "intifada" into the quiet of the night. It echoed across the entire campus, heard in every dorm. In that moment, they embodied the very spirit of resistance we had worked tirelessly to ignite. In that moment, as the rain mingled with the tears on my face, I stood there, over-whelmed. The countless hours of meticulous planning—designing flyers, timing posts to maximize turnout— had now become insignificant. The fire we had ignited had become a blazing force of its own, unstoppable and alive.

This moment marked the beginning of a new chapter in our struggle. We had crossed a threshold, fully aware of the imminent consequences. It was then that I recognized—there was no longer any fear within our collective.

On April 19, the police entered our encampment, delivering repeated warnings that we would face arrest if we did not disperse. This time, despite having summoned a picket of students, the NYPD entered our encampment. In response, we, sixty students, locked arms in a circle, resolute and unwavering, and began to sing: "We shall not be moved." We chanted, "Disclose, divest, we will not stop, we will not rest." One by one, they began arresting us. The shock was palpable as the student body erupted in cries of "Shame!" Many, witnessing their peers being arrested before their eyes, could not hold back their tears. The entire campus had gathered—students, faculty, and staff—all witnessing this moment unfold. As we were led away, our voices hoarse but unyielding, we chanted until the end. Even our legal observers were arrested. After what felt like an eternity, we were finally loaded into NYPD vans, our chants still echoing in the spaces we left behind.

The first words I heard upon leaving jail came from a friend who told me, "They occupied the second lawn."

Despite the original group of sixty students camping, 120 arrests took place that day. I later learned that, after our arrests, the students in the picket had hopped the fence to reclaim our spots as an act of defiance. Then, the onlooking students took the other lawn and began a new encampment spontaneously.

The second encampment felt fundamentally different. The distinction between those within the encampment and the broader student body had completely dissolved. The encampment was the students, and the students were the encampment.

It became, as we had hoped, a vibrant space for political education and community building. It was a space where students could leave their belongings unattended for hours without fear. There were Shabbat dinners led by Jewish student organizers, Friday prayers—where Muslim students prayed together while other students held up blankets to shield them from Zionists recording from outside—teach-ins, art, and speeches from various cultural organizations. Every day, there were daily updates from Gaza read out loud to the camp to ensure nobody lost focus. While the media attempted to portray the encampment as an antisemitic mob, anyone who visited could see that it was, in reality, a beautiful manifestation of community, learning, and care.

After two weeks of negotiations between our organizers and the administration, Columbia University President Minouche Shafik sent an email to the entire student body, explicitly stating, "We will not divest from Israel." This declaration sparked outrage across the campus. The follow-ing day, a group of students, acting autonomously, occupied Hamilton Hall, a space historically occupied during protests at Columbia. They unfurled a banner and renamed the hall "Hind's Hall" in honor of Hind Rajab, a six-year-old Palestinian girl who was killed by Israeli forces.

The following day, campus was put on lockdown, and returning became impossible as it was clear the administra-tion was preparing for a raid. That evening, the NYPD arrived in force, sealing off access and barricading journalists and EMTs inside buildings to prevent documentation of the unfolding events. The police indiscriminately beat protest-ers, leaving many severely injured. Inside Hind's Hall, offic-ers resorted to using a crane to enter through the windows after we barricaded the doors with everything available. Flash grenades were deployed while officers violently kicked protesters in the face, resulting in swollen faces and severe physical trauma. Several students suffered concussions, and one sustained a deep gash on their leg. I witnessed Muslim women having their hijabs forcibly removed in jail in front of male officers. Manhattan's district attorney later confirmed that a cop had also fired a gun inside of Hind's Hall.

When I finally had the opportunity to reflect on that night's events, the full scope of what had transpired hit me all at once. It wasn't merely an isolated incident; it was a collective trauma that reverberated throughout the entire student body. Columbia University had once again called the police on its own students, marking the second such occurrence in just two weeks. The irony was not lost on us—it was the fifty-sixth anniversary of the very day in 1968 when the university had called the police to arrest over 700 students who were protesting the Vietnam War and the gentrification of Harlem.

Elite institutions like Columbia proudly admit students based on their commitment to activism and social justice— until those students actually challenge the status quo. Columbia capitalizes on the legacies of their former student activists while actively repressing and punishing their current student activists. The same institution that capitalizes on the legacy of Edward Said was the one that called the police to mass arrest the students advocating for the very principles Said espoused. This stark contradiction reveals a simple truth: decolonization theory is only acceptable at institutions like Columbia as long as it remains confined to the realm of theory.

To attribute this repression solely to Columbia would be a grave mistake. As 127 encampments were established during this time, over 3,000 students, faculty, and staff were arrested across the US. At UCLA, students were attacked by a pro-Israel mob with pepper spray, sticks, stones, and fireworks, which left them bloody, many with severe head injuries—the police refused to intervene. At NYU, the semester after the encampments, they made "Zionist" a protected class to ensure that students who criticize the settler-colonial ideology can be disciplined for doing so. London School of Economics (LSE) took their own students to court over their encampment. University of Pennsylvania police have raided the homes of student activists.

Our battle, in the end, is not with university administrators. It is with the imperialist system that upholds this violence on our campuses and abroad in Palestine. Of course, we faced severe repression—two NYPD raids in two weeks, culminating in the arrests of over 200 students. Many students, including me, are still facing suspension. Yet, the media neglected to address the gravity of the consequences or brutality we faced, let alone the root causes behind it—the university's investments in the machinery of occupation and oppression that fueled it. Instead, the focus remains on a sanitized version of the narrative, neatly packaged to protect the status quo.

Under the settler-colonial apparatus, academic freedom is nothing more than a facade, bound to crumble. This system is not confined to isolated domains but weaves its influence throughout every aspect of our lives. It saturates our workplaces, molds the media we consume, shapes the curriculum in our classrooms, and dictates the boundaries of public discourse. These entrenched power structures define the limits of what is permissible to say, who is allowed to speak, and which narratives are granted space to grow. In a system that thrives on the preservation of capital and empire, genuine academic freedom cannot exist, for it is perpetually constrained by the very forces that seek to maintain control over knowledge, justice, and discourse.

This is why we insist that academic freedom cannot be disentangled from our call for divestment from Israel—these are inseparable issues. Should a space for learning have financial, institutional, and political ties to the Israeli occupation, when this means their primary loyalty lies in protecting the interests of those who uphold these oppressive power structures?

Palestinian journalists are sacrificing their lives to document the truth, to ensure that we all bear witness. Do you truly believe they expect nothing more than our passive sympathy? Or do they endure these unfathomable sacrifices in the hope that we will be moved to act? Time and again, we are asked why we have chosen to sacrifice so much—our education, our careers, our reputations. My question is this: How could anyone choose inaction when confronted with the most televised genocide in the world? How could anyone feel anything but the most resolute moral clarity and urgency? What worth does my Columbia degree hold if I remain silent while every university in Gaza has been turned to rubble, with the help of my tuition and tax dollars?

Genocide is the ultimate crime against humanity—the total annihilation of an entire people. A society that not only normalizes and accepts genocide but also shields it from criticism by any means is one rotting at its core. The size of our student movement is rooted in the collective understanding that the genocide in Gaza is directly connected to the struggles of all oppressed people everywhere. Fascist, settler-colonial states are watching Israel's impunity and using it as a model. In India, far-right figures now advocate for an "Israel-like solution in Kashmir," inspired by a year of atrocities. In the United States, the last year of repression shows how much violence they are willing to inflict on us in order to protect the interests of capital and empire.

Our commitment to humanity is on trial. And, right now, we are failing.

# 20

# To Khalid
*Killed on January 22, 2024, by an Israeli airstrike*

## Ahmed Masoud

Eternal is your name in Arabic
So stay immortal,
Beyond the borderlines of this world,
Beyond the pain, beyond what you have seen in Gaza
Beyond your child's screams of hunger and fear
You will be in a smokeless, bombless place,
So wait for me, brother.
Be patient and don't leave,
You are only allowed to leave once.
When I get there, I don't want to see you sad or old
Angry or tired
Scared of bombs or big tanks
Frustrated or worried
Just stay as we were
Two excited lads
Wanting to play the Oud
And cycle to the beach
I will practice playing new songs

And I will show off
In the meantime, while you wait
teach them how to sand wood
To make beautiful furniture
Or show the kids how to play marbles brilliantly
You can keep your big smile
As you busy yourself doing things for others
Like you have always done
Whatever you do, just stay there
I am coming, I won't be long

# Afterword

## *Yara Eid*

"We love life whenever we can. We dance and throw up a minaret or raise palm trees for the violets growing between two martyrs," wrote the beloved Palestinian poet Mahmoud Darwish. He proclaimed to the world what lies at the heart of Palestine: love. And in Gaza, love can be felt everywhere, even amid genocide.

When we think of the term "war," our minds naturally wander to everything that's ugly. War is torture, displacement, hunger, death, blood, and fear. War is the opposite of love. But in Gaza, despite being faced with all these horrors for over a year, love surrounds it. Love is what keeps the tiny occupied land from being wiped off the face of the earth. It is choosing to remain even as the most powerful nations try to force you out with their arms and influence.

Whenever I meet a fellow Gazan—whether a new or old acquaintance—they always speak about Gaza with that same profound emotion that outshines the ugliness and the pain.

Indeed, in Palestine it is expressed through so many of our rituals: when we commemorate our deceased; when doctors refuse to stop treating their patients even at gunpoint; when journalists fight to deliver their message despite constant threats. It is the resistance protecting their land through unimaginable conditions, the same land to which the children of Palestine are deeply attached even when they have only ever seen it in ruins.

Certainly, love is our foundation: We share a love of the fertile earth that gives us our olive trees; in every stitch of *tatreez*; in the stories of our ancestors preserved in our folk songs, and even in the mint tea we sip in front of our beach. It is heard through the *oud* played by musicians who write songs from their flimsy tents in refugee camps.

It is also in what became the everyday in Gaza, like a husband standing in line for sixteen hours to fetch clean water despite being wounded. Or families sharing their food with their neighbors when there is too little to even feed themselves.

Palestinians taught the world much as they resisted through giving life, by fighting and remaining steadfast in the face of Israel's machine—for some, even till the end.

For the Palestinian survivors I've spoken to, this is what kept them going, kept them resilient for over fifteen months of genocide.

Like the young woman who had been living in newlywed bliss with her husband—a journalist—when a missile struck their home. He stepped in front of her to shield her and was killed instantly. In the wake of his death, she took up his work, determined to honor his legacy. She is now raising their baby daughter to be brave, just like her father.

"I lost everything in this genocide: my only love, and my life somewhere along the way, " she told me. "But my husband proved in his final moments on earth that there are no obstacles to love if you decide. He was our protector and our shield from an Israeli airstrike, and preserved our lives instead of his own."

Despite the occupier's best efforts, love endures among the Palestinian people. We protect one another—including our martyrs.

You see, love has a different meaning in the middle of the genocide. This is something a young Palestinian mother told me. For seven years she had struggled to conceive another child and had three miscarriages. Her husband had struggled to get her the medication she needed, and to pay for medical bills, but somehow, she fell pregnant.

This is what helped them hang on for dear life amid all this pain and suffering, her husband explained.

The idea of trying to have another baby following miscarriages and displacement, as deadly strikes continue to rain down, is inconceivable to most on this earth. But for her it was a powerful symbol that the life growing inside her will come into the world and be raised to share the same passion for her homeland.

The stories of intimacy, eternal love, and compassion that come from Gaza are likely to be forgotten or overseen not only during the bloodshed, but also in the aftermath as questions of accountability and rebuilding are prioritised. We must therefore preserve them by recounting and documenting the intimate experiences of Palestinians.

For me, love is central to our survival as Palestinians. It is expressed when we stand together united in the face of oppression and when we refuse to give up.

This only deepens through our struggle for justice—and by continuing to speak of our homeland, so the world never forgets our story.

It is the reason I decided to go back and fight after a long year of sickness, and why I chose to write these words.

If not for the love of our land and the Palestinians it belongs to, how else would we still be alive? Why else would we still be fighting to free it?

# Acknowledgments

The editors extend their heartfelt gratitude to the Open Society Foundations, in particular the Ideas Workshop, for their generous support. We are also deeply thankful to Julia Churchill, Aliya Gulamani, Karolina Sutton, and Michal Schatz, as well as the entire team at Verso Books for their invaluable contributions. Above all, we are indebted to our contributors for entrusting us with their stories.

# Contributors

**susan abulhawa** is a novelist and poet. Her debut novel, *Mornings in Jenin*, is considered a classic in Palestinian literature. Her work has been translated into over thirty languages. The sales and linguistic reach of her books have made Abulhawa the most widely read Palestinian author of all time. She is the founder of Playgrounds for Palestine, and the Palestine Writes Literature Festival.

**Hiba Abu Nada** was a novelist, poet, and educator. Her novel *Oxygen is Not for the Dead* won the Sharjah Award for Arab Creativity in 2017. She wrote "I Grant you Refuge" on October 10, 2023. She died a martyr, killed in south Gaza by an Israeli raid on October 20, 2023. She was thirty-two years old. The poem is translated by Huda Fakhreddine, Associate Professor of Arabic literature at the University of Pennsylvania. Fakhreddine is a writer, translator, and the author of several scholarly books.

**Mosab Abu Toha** is a Palestinian poet, short story writer, and essayist from Gaza. His first collection of poetry, *Things You*

*May Find Hidden in My Ear*, was a finalist for the National
Book Critics Circle Award for Poetry and won the Palestine
Book Award, the American Book Award, and the Walcott
Poetry Prize. Abu Toha is also the founder of the Edward
Said Library in Gaza, which he hopes to rebuild. He recently
won an Overseas Press Club Award for his "Letter from
Gaza" columns for the *New Yorker*.

**Ahmed Alnaouq** is the co-founder and director of We Are
Not Numbers and a journalist with Palestine Deep Dive. He
was awarded a Chevening Scholarship to pursue a master's
degree in international journalism at the University of Leeds.
Before his current roles, he served as an advocacy and
outreach officer for the Euro-Mediterranean Human Rights
Monitor.

**Laila Al-Arian** is the executive producer of Fault Lines, a
Washington, DC–based current affairs program on Al
Jazeera English. Prior to that, she produced short documen-
taries on subjects ranging from the Muslim ban to conditions
in factories producing garments for Walmart and Gap in
Bangladesh. She has been honored with three News and
Documentary Emmys and twenty-one nominations, as well
as Peabody, George Polk, and Overseas Press Club awards.
She is the executive producer of *The Night Won't End*, a
feature-length documentary on civilian killings by the Israeli
military in Gaza. She is the co-author of *Collateral Damage:
America's War on Iraqi Civilians*.

**Tareq Baconi** is author of *Hamas Contained: A History of Palestinian Resistance* (Stanford University Press: 2018, 2024). He was the senior analyst for Palestine/Israel at the International Crisis Group, based in Ramallah. His writing has appeared in the *New York Review of Books*, the *London Review of Books*, and the *New York Times*, among others. He is president of the board of Al-Shabaka: The Palestinian Policy Network.

**Mariam Barghouti** is a Palestinian writer, researcher, and journalist who has covered the Levant as a reporter and analyst for more than a decade.

**Omar Barghouti** is a Palestinian human rights defender and co-founder of the Palestinian-led Boycott, Divestment and Sanctions (BDS) movement and the Palestinian Campaign for the Academic and Cultural Boycott of Israel (PACBI). He is a recipient of the 2017 Gandhi Peace Award. He holds a B.Sc. and an M.Sc. in Electrical Engineering from Columbia University, NY, and is pursuing a PhD in Philosophy (ethics) at the University of Amsterdam. He is the author of *BDS: The Global Struggle for Palestinian Rights* (Haymarket: 2011), and his views and opinions have been published in the *Guardian*, *Washington Post*, and *Le Monde*, among many others.

**Eman Basher** is a Gazan writer, former English teacher, and graduate assistant with a passion for storytelling and resistance through words. A mother of three, she has published work in *Vice* magazine, *Electronic Intifada*, *Washington Post*, and *Vittles*. Her writing explores Palestinian identity, history, and survival, often shaped by personal experiences and the ongoing struggle in Gaza.

**Mona Chalabi** is an award-winning writer and illustrator who uses data as the foundation for her work. By translating complex statistics, Mona has earned a Pulitzer Prize, a fellowship at the British Science Association, an Emmy nomination, and recognition from the Royal Statistical Society. In recent years, her art has been exhibited at the Smithsonian Design Museum, the Tate, the Brooklyn Museum, and the Design Museum. Her work can also be found at the *New Yorker*, *Guardian*, Netflix, NPR, BBC, and National Geographic. Mona is currently writing a book about the ways we talk about money. She is also the executive producer and creative director of an upcoming animated TV show with Ramy Youssef, A24, and Amazon Studios. She studied international relations in Paris and Arabic in Jordan.

**Yara Eid** is a Palestinian journalist and human rights advocate who has worked for international human rights organizations such as Amnesty International. She is a writer who explores the struggles of living under apartheid and occupation. Yara has worked as a war journalist and covered the 2022 aggression against Gaza from the ground. Her work has been published in *Al Jazeera*, *Los Angeles Times*, and *New Arab*, among other publications. She is most known for her heated debate with a Sky News anchor that went viral because of her strong arguments, which led to more than a million followers supporting her work on her social media platform.

**Huda J. Fakhreddine** is a writer and translator. She is the author of the creative non-fiction *ẓaman ṣaghīr taḥt shams thāniya* (A Small Time under a Different Sun, 2019) and the poetry collection *wa min thamma al-ʿālam* (And then, the world!, 2025). Among her translations are *Lighthouse for the Drowning* by Jawdat Fakhreddine (BOA Editions), *The Universe, All at Once: Selections from Salim Barakat* (Seagull Books), and *Palestinian: Poems* by Ibrahim Nasrallah (World Poetry Books). She is Associate Professor of Arabic Literature at the University of Pennsylvania, the co-editor of Middle Eastern Literatures, and the author of several scholarly books.

**Dr. Tanya Haj-Hassan** is a pediatric intensive care and humanitarian doctor. She spends half her year working with Doctors without Borders (MSF) and has served on medical missions throughout Africa and Middle East. Dr. Haj-Hassan has been visiting the West Bank and Gaza Strip for over ten years to teach medical school students alongside a group of doctors and surgeons from Oxford. As a founding member of OxPal, she has helped develop various teaching opportunities for Palestinian medical students. Throughout that time, she has built long-standing relationships with Palestinian medics and stands in awe of their commitment to their patients and profession. Dr. Haj-Hassan has been serving as a spokesperson for MSF on Gaza since October 2023. In that capacity, she has attempted to share with the world the immensity of the catastrophe that is unfolding in Gaza.

**Dr. Yara Hawari** is a writer and political commentator. She serves as co-director for Al-Shabaka: the Palestinian Policy Network. Yara completed her PhD in Middle East Politics at the University of Exeter in 2017 which focused on Indigenous oral history in Palestine. She published her first novel, *The Stone House* (Hajar Press), in 2021 and is the host of the podcast Rethinking Palestine.

**Maryam Iqbal** is an organizer with Columbia Students for Justice in Palestine and an aspiring journalist. A sophomore at Barnard College studying Middle Eastern studies, she was suspended through the fall semester of 2024 for her involvement in the Gaza Solidarity Encampment. She dedicates her contribution to the brave and steadfast journalists of Palestine who have paid the ultimate price for epitomizing the truest principles of journalism and showing the world the reality, for being the ultimate guiding compass for journalists of conscience, and for showing the world that occupation doesn't leave us voiceless—it leaves us unheard.

**Nina Lakhani** has been a reporter for almost two decades focused on exposing injustice around the world including land struggles, the battle for natural resources, state sponsored repression, and gender-based violence. She has reported from over a dozen countries, including seven years freelancing in Mexico and Central America, and is currently a senior reporter for the *Guardian*. She's the author of *Who Killed Berta Cáceres? Dams, Death Squads, and an Indigenous Defender's Battle for the Planet*. Before journalism she was a mental health nurse.

**Ahmed Masoud** is the author of the acclaimed novels *Vanished: The Mysterious Disappearance of Mustafa Ouda* and *Come What May*. Ahmed is a writer, poet, and director who grew up in Gaza, Palestine, and moved to the UK in 2002. Ahmed's theatre and radio drama credits include: *The Florist of Rafah* (2024), *Passports, Jinn, Mo Salah and Other Complicated Things* (2023), *Application 39* (WDR Radio, Germany, 2018) *Camouflage* (London, 2017), *The Shroud Maker* (London, 2015—still touring), *Walaa, Loyalty* (London, 2014, funded by the Arts Council England), *Escape from Gaza* (BBC Radio 4, 2011), ahmedmasoud.co.uk.

**Lina Mounzer** is a Lebanese writer and translator. Her work has appeared in the *Paris Review*, *Freeman's*, *Washington Post*, and the *Baffler*, as well as in the anthologies *Tales of Two Planets* (Penguin, 2020) and *Best American Essays 2022* (Harper Collins, 2022). She is senior editor at the literary arts and culture magazine the *Markaz Review*.

**Noor Alyacoubi** is a translator and writer deeply committed to sharing the untold stories of war and its devastating impact on innocent lives. Through her work, she strives to shine a light on the atrocities of war, both personal and collective. Noor is the daughter of a loving family, whom she last saw in October 2023, and a mother to a young child who was just six months old when the war began. For the past fifteen months, she has endured the harsh realities of displacement, famine, fear, and terror in the devastated northern Gaza.

**Joe Sacco**, one of the world's greatest cartoonists, is widely hailed as the creator of war reportage comics. He is the author of, among other books, *Palestine*, which received the American Book Award, and *Safe Area Goražde*, which won the Eisner Award and was named a *New York Times* notable book and *Time* magazine's best comic book of 2000. His books have been translated into fourteen languages, and his comics reporting has appeared in *Details*, *New York Times Magazine*, *Time*, *Harper's*, and *Guardian*. He lives in Portland, Oregon.

**Shareef Sarhan** (b. 1976, Gaza) is a visual artist and photographer. He is a founding member of Shababeek for Contemporary Art and an active member of the Association of Palestinian Artists. Sarhan earned his diploma in art and was a participant in the Darat Al Funun academy in Jordan. His work has garnered several accolades, including a recognition award in 2007 and the Bronze Award from the Festival of Arab Photographers in 2008. He is also the creator of the picture book *Gaza Live*. Sarhan's art has been exhibited in Gaza, Ramallah, Jerusalem, Amman, and internationally in the United States, France, Germany, and Italy.

**Dr. Malaka Shwaikh** is a Palestinian academic based at the University of St. Andrews (Scotland). She has over seven years of experience in academic and consultancy roles, working at the intersection of prison studies, hunger strikes, peacebuilding, and resilience. Her mission is to challenge dominant narratives and practices of peace and conflict studies, and to contribute to the decolonization of knowledge production and dissemination. She is also a trustee of local organizations that support mental health and education for under-privileged communities. She co-founded Freelancersin Gaza.com (2021) to connect Gaza youths with clients around the world and provide them with mentorship.

**Mary Turfah** is a writer and resident physician. Her work has appeared in the *Baffler*, *LA Review of Books*, *Bookforum*, and elsewhere.